PRAISE FOR
THE ART OF SELLING YOUR BUSINESS

"If selling our business was like climbing Mount Everest, then *The Art of Selling Your Business: Winning Strategies & Secret Hacks for Exiting on Top* is like the ultimate sherpa to get you to the top."

—Damien James, Founder
SOLD DIMPLE FOR $13.4 MILLION

"Jam-packed with negotiation secrets. Should be required reading for anyone considering selling their business."

—Dan Martell, Founder
THREE SUCCESSFUL EXITS

"In *The Art of Selling Your Business*, John shares incisive, practical advice on how to best develop companies for this high-value milestone. A compelling read!"

—Aurangzeb Khan, Founder
SOLD ALTIA SYSTEMS TO JABRA GN FOR $125 MILLION

"During a negotiation to monetize all that work you've done to build your business, you can lose years of equity value in minutes if you are not prepared. *The Art of Selling Your Business* is a must-read (and apply) now to ensure full value for your business."

—Michael Houlihan, Co-Founder and *NYT* best-selling author, *The Barefoot Spirit*
SOLD BAREFOOT WINES TO EJ GALLO

The ART of SELLING YOUR BUSINESS

WINNING STRATEGIES & SECRET
HACKS FOR EXITING ON TOP

JOHN WARRILLOW

AN INC.
ORIGINAL

An Inc. Original
New York, New York
www.anincoriginal.com

This work is being published under the An Inc. Original imprint by an exclusive
arrangement with *Inc.* magazine. *Inc.* magazine and the Inc. logo are registered
trademarks of Mansueto Ventures, LLC. The An Inc. Original logo is a wholly
owned trademark of Mansueto Ventures, LLC.

Distributed by Greenleaf Book Group

For ordering information or special discounts for bulk purchases, please contact
Greenleaf Book Group at PO Box 91869, Austin, TX 78709, 512.891.6100.

Design and composition by Greenleaf Book Group
Cover design by Greenleaf Book Group

Publisher's Cataloging-in-Publication data is available.
Print ISBN: 978-1-7334781-5-1

eBook ISBN: 978-1-7334781-6-8

Part of the Tree Neutral® program, which offsets the number of trees consumed in
the production and printing of this book by taking proactive steps, such as planting
trees in direct proportion to the number of trees used: www.treeneutral.com

Printed in the United States of America on acid-free paper

20 21 22 23 24 25 26   10 9 8 7 6 5 4 3 2 1

First Edition

I'm not a lawyer. Nor am I an accountant, a financial advisor, or a mergers and acquisitions (M&A) professional. Therefore, please treat the opinions here as just that: opinions. They are not, and should not be treated as, professional advice. Selling your business is not a do-it-yourself project. You should have your own team of experts advising you on the most important transaction of your life. Hire the best you can afford. They'll be worth every penny.

My apologies in advance to the M&A professionals, corporate finance attorneys, and business brokers who consider this book an over-simplification of a complex process. My goal is not to "dumb down" your work, but simply to focus on the important bits that owners need to know and to package those bits in a format that (hopefully) doesn't read too much like a textbook. At times, I'm sure I will frustrate you by glossing over critical details and technicalities. I tried to illustrate both the forest and the trees, but no doubt missed in places.

AN IMPORTANT NOTE BEFORE YOU START

Before you start reading, please download *The Art of Selling Your Business* Workbook (it's free). I designed the workbook with exercises from each chapter, so you can apply what you are learning to your business. You'll also get some other goodies, such as a free chapter of *Built to Sell* and a new episode of *Built to Sell Radio* each week. Just pop your email address into the form at BuiltToSell.com.

CONTENTS

Contents

SECTION 1

Things to Consider Before You Start

Think of selling your business as a long, tough journey into the back-country. You will encounter plenty of obstacles, but if you pack right, you'll be fine. Consider this section an essential list of things you need to arrange before starting your trek.

Chapter 1

VALUE *IS* IN THE EYE OF THE ACQUIRER

I'm not much of an artist, but if you gave me a can of white paint, I could probably make a close replica.

It's called *Bridge*, but it's just a square white canvas, painted all white. It was created by the late Robert Ryman, who was apparently a big deal in the contemporary art world. He was known for something called minimalism, which became a thing in the 1960s.

To me, it just looks like a white ceiling tile that was removed from a high school cafeteria. That's why I find it so shocking that someone would pay $20.6 million for *Bridge* at a Christie's auction.[1]

But here's the thing: I know nothing about art. If I weren't such a Neanderthal, I might appreciate the value of an original canvas from one of the 20th century's most prolific artists.

But I don't.

And that's okay because someone does—in fact, a lot of people do.

One person's ceiling tile is another person's masterpiece. Similarly, your business can be worth different amounts depending on whom you're asking. Sure, you can probably look up a standard industry benchmark for valuing your company, but you can also look up the cost of a white ceiling tile.

There's an art to selling a business well. It comes down to how you package it, the story you tell about it, and the feeling it gives potential buyers when they imagine owning it. As you'll see in chapter 16, it's how Gary Miller got IBM to almost quadruple its acquisition offer for Aragon Consulting Group from three times earnings before interest, taxes, depreciation, and amortization (EBITDA) to almost *11* times.[2] It's the same reason Stephanie Breedlove sold her $9 million payroll company for $54 million[3] (also covered in chapter 16).

---

1 "Post-War and Contemporary Art Evening Sale, New York," Christies.com, May 13, 2015, https://www.christies.com/lotfinder/Lot/robert-ryman-b-1930-bridge-5896026-details.aspx

2 John Warrillow, "How to Handle a Low-Ball Offer," *Built to Sell Radio*, podcast, January 4, 2019, https://builttosell.com/radio/episode-163/

3 John Warrillow, "Would You Have the Audacity to Turn Down $40MM for a $9MM Company?," *Built to Sell Radio*, podcast, December 21, 2016, https://builttosell.com/radio/episode-74/

There is a systematic way to calculate the value of your company—but if you're all head and no heart, you will miss the point.

The Art of Selling Your Business is designed to be your playbook for navigating both the hard rules and the softer edges of selling well. It features a set of instructions to follow at each step of the process and describes the professionals you'll need to lean on to get a deal done.

MY STORY

I've started and exited a few small businesses, and I've tried to describe what I have learned about making them valuable in a book I wrote called *Built to Sell: Creating a Business That Can Thrive Without You*, which was published in 2011. In 2015, I wrote a companion book called *The Automatic Customer: Creating a Subscription Business in Any Industry*, which illustrates how to create a recurring revenue model—one of the value drivers I covered in *Built to Sell*.

The books led to my creating a company called The Value Builder System™, where our community of approximately 1,000 Certified Value Builders™ have helped more than 50,000 business owners maximize the value of their business.

Based on my experience running The Value Builder System and writing a couple of books on the topic of building to sell, I occasionally get asked to speak to groups of entrepreneurs. My standard talk covers eight things acquirers look for when they evaluate your company as a potential acquisition—for example, how fast your company is likely to grow in the future, how much recurring revenue you have, how well you have differentiated your product or service, and how dependent your business is on your personal involvement.

Interestingly, the questions I get from a typical audience have less to do with my speech and more to do with the details of negotiating the sale of a business. Instead of theoretical questions about the drivers of value in a small business, I get asked stuff like:

- "How do I avoid an earnout?"
- "How do I let potential buyers know I'm interested in selling, without looking desperate?"
- "When should I tell my employees I'm thinking of selling?"
- "How can I create a bidding war for my company?"
- "What do I do when a potential buyer wants me to sign a 'no-shop clause'?"
- "How do I handle a potential acquirer who wants to talk to my employees and customers as a part of their due diligence?"

Because these questions are around the *mechanics* of selling rather than the theories of building value, I began to realize that there was a need for impartial advice on how to go about negotiating the sale of a business.

THE BIRTH OF *BUILT TO SELL RADIO*

These post-talk Q&A sessions led me to see that business owners want actionable advice on selling their businesses, which inspired me to launch a podcast called *Built to Sell Radio,* where I interview a different founder every week and ask them about the sale of their business. Rather than have them explain how they got started, or how they grew their business, I focus my questions on their exit:

- "What triggered you to consider selling?"
- "How did you find a buyer?"
- "What was the negotiation like?"
- "How much did you get for your business?"
- "What were the deal's terms?"
- "What proportion of your payment is at risk in an earnout?"
- "What was the most unexpected thing you got asked for during diligence?"
- "What would you do differently if you could negotiate the sale of your business all over again?"

This collection of hundreds of interviews with cashed-out entrepreneurs has become a treasure trove of techniques, hacks, ideas, negotiation strategies, and lessons learned about selling a small business, which I decided to amalgamate—along with my own personal experience—into this book.

The Art of Selling Your Business is not about how to start a business. There's plenty out there on getting going. It's also not about how to create a valuable company; that was my focus in *Built to Sell* and *The Automatic Customer*. Instead, this book assumes you already have a successful company and you're trying to figure out how to sell it for a decent price.

I'm not talking about selling assets like your inventory and equipment—any auctioneer can get rid of your stuff. Instead, I'll be talking about maximizing what accountants call "goodwill," which is the difference between the market value of your business and the current value of your hard assets. The art of selling your business is getting someone to value something they cannot touch. In essence, they are buying a story about what your business could be in their hands.

I'm also not focused on companies with less than $1 million in annual revenue, which typically sell to an individual for a modest multiple of seller's discretionary earnings (SDE).[4] If you have a six-figure company, you may take something away from this book, but the process of selling a Main Street business involves listing it for sale like you might list a property, which takes away much of the art of selling well.

Instead, *The Art of Selling Your Business* is for the owner of a company worth somewhere between $1 million and $50 million, where the art form has the biggest impact. Unlike the sale of larger businesses in transparent auctions where acquirers often disclose deal terms to their shareholders, the sale of a business worth between $1 million and $50 million is shrouded in mystery. Details are hidden behind the nondisclosure agreements (NDAs) that sellers are required to sign, leaving us few examples to follow in order to navigate the treacherous waters of selling a business.

---

4 This is a formula business brokers use to calculate the economic benefit you derive from owning your business, such as your profit; your salary; bonuses you pay yourself; and any other benefits you receive from your business with an economic value, including car payments, travel, etc.

I've divided the book into three distinct sections, which correspond to the process you'll go through to sell your business:

1. Section 1 tackles some things to do before you start—consider it an essential packing list before you set out on your journey to sell.

2. Section 2 looks at how to create negotiating leverage by drumming up multiple offers.

3. Section 3 provides a recipe for coming out on top in a negotiation to sell your business.

Before we dive into soliciting acquisition offers and the dark art of negotiation, there is one essential question you need to answer first.

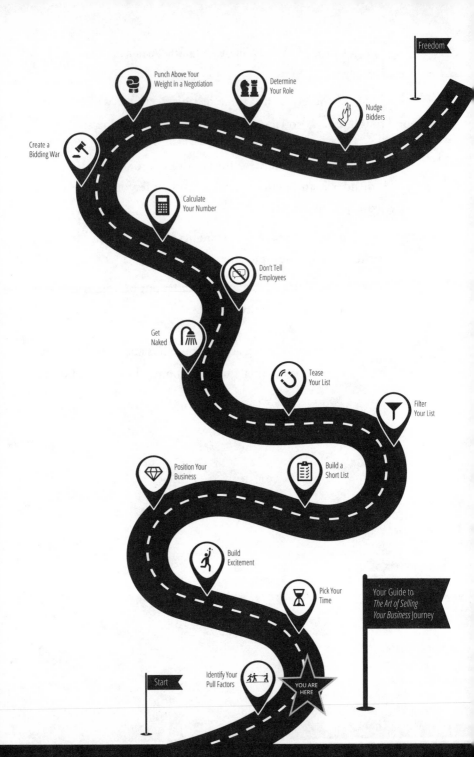

Freedom

Punch Above Your
Weight in a Negotiation

Determine
Your Role

Nudge
Bidders

Create a
Bidding War

Calculate
Your Number

Don't Tell
Employees

Get
Naked

Tease
Your List

Filter
Your List

Position Your
Business

Build a
Short List

Build
Excitement

Pick Your
Time

Your Guide to
*The Art of Selling
Your Business* Journey

Identify Your
Pull Factors

YOU ARE
HERE

Start

This map is intended as a visual representation of the journey you'll take to sell your business. You can also download *The Art of Selling Your Business*

Chapter 2

The Secret to a Happy Exit

THE MOST IMPORTANT QUESTION
MOST FOUNDERS NEVER ANSWER

Turning 30 is a big deal.

Leaving our 20s behind and turning 30 is one of those milestone events that causes most of us to engage in a bit of self-reflection. For Colorado-based Shaun Oshman, that 30th birthday triggered a unique response. Oshman decided to cut out a set of pictures that symbolized where he wanted to be by the age of 40 and pinned them to a corkboard as a reminder.

Ten years is a perfect time horizon for a vision board because, unlike shorter-term goals, 10 years allows you to imagine something really big. Accordingly, Oshman pinned a picture of a sailboat on his board, which was intended to remind him of his goal for the decade: design a life that would allow him to be living on a yacht by his 40th birthday.

Soon after his board was complete, Oshman set about making his vision a reality. He started a small IT services business called iSupportU. If you lived in Boulder in the early 2000s and wanted to install antivirus software, collaborate with a team using technology, or lace together a few computers into a network at your office, Oshman was your man.

The business went through the normal growing pains of a young start-up, eventually reaching a few million dollars in annual sales. As Oshman's 39th birthday approached, he started to ready the company for sale, knowing that he would need to exit in order to fulfill his vision of a life on the high seas.

To get iSupportU exit-ready, Oshman started focusing on selling more IT services with a recurring revenue model. Next, Oshman hired someone as head of business development to replace himself as the rainmaker for his company. Finally, Oshman started to take off one week out of every month to see how his business would run when he was not in the office, returning to fix any cracks that formed in his absence.

Soon after his 39th birthday, Oshman figured the time was right to sell and hired a broker to drum up some offers. Within three months, Oshman's broker had received five solid bids for iSupportU, ranging from two to three times SDE. Oshman felt a great cultural fit with one individual bidder and quickly agreed to terms.

When I last spoke to Oshman,[5] he was happy as a clam, having accepted nearly three times SDE for his business. He was building his spearfishing skills and living on his yacht.

He had just celebrated his 40th birthday.

Three times profit may not sound like a great result—in fact, according to our research over at The Value Builder System, it's pretty average for a small services company.

So why is Oshman so happy?

He's satisfied because he wasn't just leaving his business; he was going *toward* something new. Oshman didn't hate his business when he sold it; he liked what he was doing and the people he worked with. But the allure of living life on a sailboat was so powerful that it trumped any sense of loss he felt after selling.

WHAT'S DRIVING YOUR DECISION TO CONSIDER SELLING YOUR BUSINESS NOW?

Are you ready to retire? Maybe a little tired? Bored? Burnt out? Sick of dealing with employees and red tape?

These are all legitimate reasons to want to sell, but if they are the *only* reasons you're leaving, you could end up regretting your decision. You've worked hard to build your business. It probably gives you a sense of purpose and accomplishment. Selling means you risk losing all of that. My friend and colleague Bo Burlingham wrote a wonderful

---

5   John Warrillow, "How a Vision Board Drove One Owner to Sell," *Built to Sell Radio*, podcast, July 5, 2017, https://builttosell.com/radio/episode-99/

book about the emotional toll of selling a business, called *Finish Big*. I'd recommend reading that book if you want to explore this topic further.

This book, however, is about the art of selling well, and we will cover lots of negotiation strategies and tactics for maximizing your take from the sale of your business. But indulge me for a minute as we address something underneath all that. One of the most important things you can do to ensure you sell your business well has nothing to do with how much money you get for your company, but it has everything to do with your reasons for wanting to sell in the first place.

PUSH VS. PULL

Most people would have you believe starting and growing a business is personal but selling is simply a business transaction. Yet selling your business is just as personal. The secret to looking back on your exit with fond memories rather than with regret is to get clear on your "pull factors."

Pull factors are the things that you're excited to go do next. What are you enthusiastic about diving into after you sell your business? That's the most important question underlying this entire process—yet most founders never ask it.

By contrast, "push factors" are the things that are pushing you out of your business. Push factors can be anything that frustrates you about your company or takes a mental toll over time.

For example, Tommy Berretz co-founded Texas Aquatic Enterprises (TAE) in 2005 to maintain commercial swimming pools for homeowners associations, water parks, apartment buildings, and schools. Once contracted, TAE managed all aspects of a community swimming pool, including construction, balancing chemicals, repairs, and hiring lifeguards.

The business grew to more than 200 employees, but by 2012, something was gnawing at Berretz. He had heard a statistic from an industry guru who said swimming pool management companies experience a drowning every seven years. Berretz had been in business for 12 years without a major incident. The thought of a child dying in a swimming pool under his management weighed heavily on Berretz and was a contributing push factor in his decision to sell TAE in 2017.[6]

As with Berretz, push factors can be fine motivators, but the secret to avoiding a feeling of loss when you sell is to get clear about your pull factors too—like Shaun Oshman envisioning life on his sailboat.

TAKING ACTION

Create your own vision board that illustrates where you want to be after you sell. Cut pictures from magazines that symbolize the things you're excited to go do, and pin them to a board. Hang your vision board prominently in your home so both you and your family can be reminded of why you're going through the process of selling your company.

---

6   John Warrillow, "How Re-Modelling A Swimming Pool Business Led To A 7-Figure Exit," *Built to Sell Radio*, podcast, August 23, 2019, https://builttosell.com/radio/episode-195/

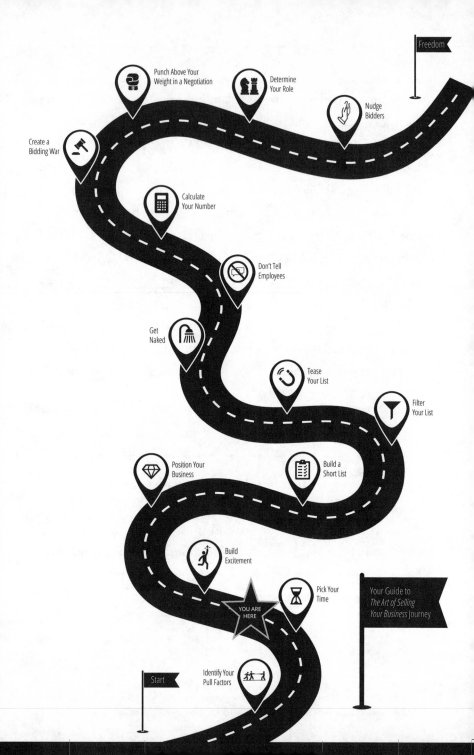

Freedom

Punch Above Your Weight in a Negotiation

Determine Your Role

Nudge Bidders

Create a Bidding War

Calculate Your Number

Don't Tell Employees

Get Naked

Tease Your List

Filter Your List

Position Your Business

Build a Short List

Build Excitement

YOU ARE HERE

Pick Your Time

Your Guide to
The Art of Selling Your Business Journey

Start

Identify Your Pull Factors

This map is intended as a visual representa[...] so download *The Art of Selling Your Business* Workbook (it's free), which I designed with [...] arning to your business. Just pop your email address into the form at BuiltToSell.com.

Chapter 3

THE DANGER OF TIMING YOUR EXIT

HOW TO DECIDE WHEN TO SELL

Fudging the books has always been frowned upon by lawmakers, but the failure of both Enron and WorldCom was a new low in American business, ushering in an era of more rigorous audit and financial requirements for public companies. In 2002, the United States passed new legislation known as the Sarbanes-Oxley Act, which (among other changes) forced big companies to do a better job archiving old email.

An ocean away, in the small town of Wellington, New Zealand, an entrepreneur named Rod Drury smelled an opportunity.

Drury reasoned large companies would now be ill-equipped to deal with the email they needed to archive, so he created After-mail, a software program that provided a better way for companies to store old emails. He targeted large, global businesses for his application and successfully signed up a handful of Fortune 500 companies, building his annual revenue to approximately $2 million in US dollars.[7]

At this point, most founders would have taken their initial success and doubled down, growing as fast as possible with the goal of capturing the maximum amount of market share and selling the company at the peak of an economic cycle. But Drury, knowing there was a lot of risk associated with trying to dominate a new market as an independent software company, chose a different tactic.

He approached Quest Software, which already had most of the Fortune 500 as clients, and together they reasoned that Quest was in the best position to benefit from what Drury had created. A few weeks later, Quest acquired Aftermail for a reported $35 million.[8]

Aftermail had yet to celebrate its third birthday.

---

7   In 2002, the US dollar was worth about twice as much, on average, as the New Zealand dollar.

8   Although *Computerworld* reported the sale price as $35 million in US dollars, when I interviewed Drury for *Built to Sell Radio* he said the founders of Aftermail actually received $14.7 million up front plus the *potential* for another $20 million if they hit their earnout targets. As you'll read in chapter 15, Drury left Quest before he became eligible to receive any proceeds from his earnout.

RIDING IT OVER THE TOP

The opposite of selling early in your life cycle, as Rod Drury did with Aftermail, is waiting too long—which is something Rand Fishkin found out in the most painful way.

Fishkin started his entrepreneurial journey when he joined his mother's marketing agency as a partner. Fishkin realized how much his mom's customers were struggling to get Google to display their company in a search, so he immersed himself in the emerging field of search engine optimization (SEO).

In addition to helping clients with their SEO, Fishkin began writing a blog called *SEO Moz*, which led to the founding of an SEO consulting and software company called Moz. By 2007, when Moz was generating revenue of $850,000 a year, Fishkin decided to drop consulting to become solely a software business.

The company began to grow 100% per year. By 2010, Moz was generating around $650,000 in revenue *each month*, attracting the attention of a variety of investors and acquirers, including Brian Halligan, co-founder of marketing software giant HubSpot.

HubSpot wanted to buy Moz and was offering $25 million in cash and HubSpot stock—an offer almost five times Moz's $5.7 million of revenue in its last complete financial year.

But Fishkin wasn't satisfied. He believed a fast-growth software-as-a-service (or SaaS) company was worth around four times future revenue and was confident Moz would hit $10 million by the end of that year. So Fishkin counteroffered, saying he would be willing to accept $40 million.

Halligan declined.

Instead of selling Moz, Fishkin raised a round of venture capital and started to diversify away from SEO tools into a broader set of marketing offerings. The adoption of Moz's new applications was weaker than he expected. The further Fishkin veered away from his core in SEO, the more money his business began to lose.

By 2014, Moz was in full crisis mode, and Fishkin had begun suffering from a bout of depression. He decided to step down as CEO, later describing his resignation in his book *Lost and Founder: A Painfully Honest Field Guide to the Startup World* as "a lot of sadness, a heap of regrets, and a smattering of resentment."

Fishkin became a minority shareholder in a company he no longer controlled, where the venture capitalists had preferred rights in a liquidity event.[9]

When I interviewed Fishkin for *Built to Sell Radio*, he estimated his liquid net worth to be around $800,000—much of which he was about to spend on elder care for his grandparents.[10] The Moz stock he holds may or may not have value after the venture capitalists get their preferred return.

Not selling when he could have done so cost Fishkin dearly. Based on the increased value of HubSpot's stock, Fishkin estimates HubSpot's offer of $25 million in cash and stock could now be worth more than $100 million.

---

9   Preferred shares have priority over common stock in the payment of dividends and upon a liquidation event (i.e., company sale). Depending on the structure, a preferred share can come with a built-in return for a holder, which has to be funded before common stockholders are paid and can wipe out the value of common stock if there is nothing left after paying out the preferred shareholders. This is how some venture-backed founders end up with little or nothing even after they sell their company.

10   John Warrillow, "How to Lose $200 Million," *Built to Sell Radio*, podcast, February 4, 2019, https://builttosell.com/radio/episode-168/

DECIDING WHEN TO SELL

If you're like a lot of founders, you're probably trying to time the sale of your business when it peaks and coincides with the top of an economic cycle.

On the surface, timing your exit seems to make sense. If you speak with mergers and acquisitions professionals, they'll tell you that an economic cycle can impact valuations by up to "two turns," which means that a business selling for five times earnings at the peak of an economic cycle may go for as low as three times earnings at a low point in the economy.

The problem is, when you sell your business, you have to do something with the money you receive, which usually means buying into another asset class that is being affected by the same economy. Sure, you may diversify a bit, but most asset classes you'll consider—from residential real estate to stocks to vacation property—generally move in the same direction as the economy.

PEAK SELLER VS. TROUGH SELLER

For example, let's compare two hypothetical sellers. Seller A and Seller B have identical businesses in the same industry, both generating $100,000 in pretax profit leading up to the Great Recession of 2008. To keep things simple, let's imagine they were both living in a country that required no tax to be paid on the sale of a business. (A guy can dream, can't he?)

Seller A sat stealthily on the sideline until the economy reached the absolute peak and sold his business for $500,000 (five times pretax profit) in October 2007. Seller A then took his $500,000 and bought into a Dow Jones index fund when it was trading above 14,000. Eighteen months later—after the Dow Jones had dropped below 7,000—Seller A would be left with less than half of his money.

Even though Seller A cleverly waited until the peak of the economic cycle, by March 9, 2009, having invested in the index, he would have effectively sold his business for less than 2.5 times earnings and would be left with less than $250,000 from the proceeds of his sale.

At first glance, Seller B waited too long and sold her business in early 2009—the trough, or lowest possible point, in the economic cycle—and got only three times earnings: $300,000. Yet notice that even in the trough, Seller B got 20% *more* than if she had sold at the peak like Seller A and bought an index fund at the top of the market.

The Seller A scenario is just like selling your house in a good real estate market; unless you're downsizing, you usually buy into an equally frothy market. When you sell, you can't put your money under your mattress, which is why timing the sale of your business on external economic cycles is usually a waste of energy.[11]

The other reason market timing is usually a mistake is that in most cases, you will have to help the new owner by staying on for a few years. Whether you sell to an individual, a private equity group (PEG), or a strategic acquirer, most deals will leave some of your money tied to future performance of your company. An individual

---

11 Although rare, the one exception to this rule is if you are in an industry that is consolidating quickly, where major players are snapping up your competitors in a race to tie up market share. Under this scenario, it may make sense to time your exit to ensure you are not the only independent company remaining in your sector after the major acquirers have finished their buying spree.

investor will need you to finance some of the purchase price; a private equity investor will usually ask you to hold on to some equity; and a strategic acquirer will often use an "earnout," where some of your money is tied to hitting goals in the future.

Regardless of how your deal is structured, you don't want to navigate a transitional period in the teeth of a recession.

DEAL MOMENTUM AND THE PRE-DILIGENCE PROCESS

If timing your exit based on economic factors is a zero-sum game, how do you figure out when to sell? The answer is to wait until your company is on a winning streak and you have the data to ensure you can create something called "deal momentum." Every transaction has a tempo to it—disrupt the pace, and you risk sabotaging your sale.

What causes a deal's cadence to be interrupted? The primary culprit is a seller who has not taken the time to assemble the information an acquirer will need during due diligence. When an excited acquirer asks for a piece of information, and you can't immediately give it to them, a little bit of their enthusiasm for the deal is lost. Fumble too many information requests, and the acquirer may lose patience and walk.

This is why you need to pull together a package of information—a process known as "pre-diligence"—detailing the essential elements of your business even before you start the process of selling it.

Now, if you're anything like me, you think of due diligence as a necessary evil and something you'll think about *if* you get an acquisition offer.

I get it.

You don't want to go to the trouble of assembling a bunch of information if there's a chance you won't need it.

This inclination toward improvising on the fly is what makes you successful as an entrepreneur. You like to dip your toe in the water before diving in.

While your instinct of hedging is absolutely right when *running* your company, it's the wrong thing to do when selling it. Once you decide to sell, you will trigger a sequence of events that are hard to walk back from.

As they say, it's like bread: you can't un-toast it.

You're going to try to keep the fact that you're selling confidential for as long as possible, but at some point, your employees, suppliers, and competitors may find out—and when they do, it will be disruptive.

That's why you don't want to put your business on the market to "test the waters." It's not like a house or a car, where you can remove it from the market without much consequence if you don't get your price. If you try to sell your business unsuccessfully, your company's value will likely be damaged in the process—perhaps irrevocably. The people your business relies on will wonder how committed you are and may forever treat you differently as a result.

The opposite of deal momentum is "deal fatigue," when everyone gets so tired of the transaction that both sides question why they're doing it. To avoid this potentially fatal malaise, you need to try to anticipate the questions a buyer will ask by assembling everything you need to answer *before* you go to market.

Imagine you're about to go on a camping trip deep into the bush.

There will be no cell reception, and you'll be a day's hike away from a paved road. Your job is to anticipate everything you might need and pack accordingly. The same is true when you are performing pre-diligence.

Do an online search for a "pre-diligence checklist," and you'll see lots of examples. You will want to get the bulk of this stuff together before you go to market. Some items are meant for larger companies, but hopefully you get the idea that a pre-diligence project is not something you want to undertake yourself. Outsource it to a consultant or your accountant.

HOW BAREFOOT WINE CREATED DEAL MOMENTUM

The other benefit of a professionally prepared pre-diligence package is that it signals to a buyer that you are serious about selling and creates the illusion of competition.

I had the opportunity to interview Michael Houlihan and Bonnie Harvey, the co-founders of Barefoot Cellars and makers of Barefoot Wine.[12] They told me that they had grown Barefoot to 600,000 cases per year when they decided it was time to sell.

The Barefoot partners put E. & J. Gallo Winery, America's largest winemaker, on their short list of potential acquirers. Gallo was much larger than Barefoot, so Houlihan and Harvey

---

12 John Warrillow, "The Backstory Behind E&J Gallo's Acquisition of Barefoot Cellars," *Built to Sell Radio*, podcast, November 22, 2019, https://builttosell.com/radio/episode-208/

knew they would only have one shot at capturing the attention of the winery's top brass.

Instead of approaching Gallo right away, the two founders prepared their pre-diligence package. Houlihan explained their rationale: "You have to do your acquirer's due diligence for them. You have to have a package for legal, HR, production, marketing, sales, and so on. These packages are going to be laid out on the table in front of them, and they are going to be given a period of time to review those packages."

Houlihan continued, "When they see that you're prepared like that, and they know they have the right of first refusal, you've created a silent auction, because if they don't take [your business], they know that you're dressed for success. They know you can take it to their biggest competitor, and you are ready to go."

On January 14, 2005, Gallo announced their acquisition of Barefoot Cellars. Deal terms were not disclosed.

A professionally prepared pre-diligence package is a subtle but powerful way to create competitive tension for your business—even if none exists.

TAKING ACTION

Stop obsessing over the perfect time to sell your business. Instead of focusing on external factors like the economy, the stock market, or interest rates, focus on your business.

Sell when the trajectory of your company is on the upswing and there's lots of excitement about the future.

Protect your deal momentum by assembling a pre-diligence package of information before you go to market. Consider outsourcing the work to an accountant or a consultant.

Building Your Negotiating Leverage

Structuring a successful sale of your business is about maximizing your leverage, and nothing allows you to negotiate with more confidence than multiple bidders vying for your company. This section will teach you how to drum up interest from potential acquirers without looking desperate.

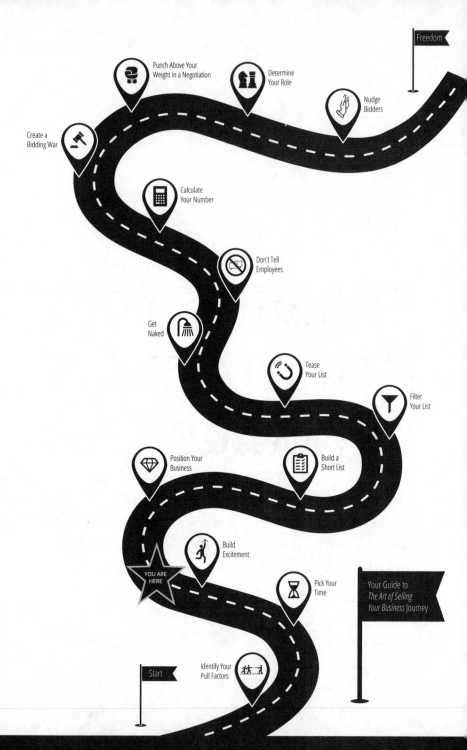

Freedom

Punch Above Your Weight in a Negotiation

Determine Your Role

Nudge Bidders

Create a Bidding War

Calculate Your Number

Don't Tell Employees

Get Naked

Tease Your List

Filter Your List

Position Your Business

Build a Short List

Build Excitement

YOU ARE HERE

Pick Your Time

Your Guide to *The Art of Selling Your Business* Journey

Start

Identify Your Pull Factors

This map is intended as a visual representation of the journey you'll take to sell your business. You can also download *The Art of Selling Your Business*

Chapter 4

THE SLOW REVEAL

How to Keep Control
of the Process

As a form of art, burlesque has been around since the fifth century B.C., when some horny artist named Aristophanes wrote a play called *Lysistrata*, in which the wives of the Athenian soldiers hole up in the Acropolis, depriving their husbands of sex until the end of the Peloponnesian War.[13] The women teased their husbands, guiding their minds toward sex, and then locked themselves away until the fighters proved their manhood by winning the war.

---

13   Dita von Teese, "A brief history of burlesque," *The Independent*, March 25, 2006, https://www.independent.co.uk/arts-entertainment/theatre-dance/features/a-brief-history-of-burlesque-471288.html

Burlesque became a form of political satire in the 17th century and then took a seedy turn into the modern-day striptease, made infamous at Las Vegas strip clubs like Cheetahs and Chippendales.

A captivating striptease provides a clear (admittedly a little crude) metaphor for the art of selling your business, which requires a slow reveal of information as the interested party becomes more aroused at the idea of what's still left to be shown. Reveal too much, too early, and some buyers may lose interest. Others may place a value, even subconsciously, on your business long before you have romanced them with your entire story. Once a value has been calculated in the acquirer's mind, it may be more difficult to get them to reprice your business later.

Just like a stripper, you must be in control of the dance that is selling your business. You decide when to reveal a new piece of information, and you never relinquish control of the process to the interested parties.

As we'll cover in the chapters that follow, your dance will start when your intermediary[14] prepares a "teaser" document that reveals just enough about your business to tempt a group of buyers to sign an NDA. Once the NDA is signed, you'll reveal a little more—including your financials and your vision for the future—in a detailed information package called a confidential information memorandum, or CIM (pronounced "sim").[15] Then you'll meet with potential acquirers, divulging even more about you and your team.

---

14 "Intermediary" is a fancy word for a business broker or an M&A professional, which you'll need (and which we'll talk about in greater detail in chapter 13).

15 Sometimes also referred to as a CIP, or confidential information presentation.

For now, I just want you to remember that information about your company is a form of currency, and as with money, you need to decide how to spend it.

This slow trickle of material is designed to protect you and to maximize the desire among a group of bidders so they all begin fighting over you at the same time. The stakes are high, and giving away vital information too early in the process can end in disaster.

In one example I have firsthand knowledge of, a PEG decided to enter a new industry and identified 80 of the leading companies in the sector. The PEG arranged meetings with each ownership team and presented each with an attractive yet vague acquisition offer. The private equity firm was careful to avoid signing an NDA, yet they held exhaustive meetings with each company's leadership team under the guise of an acquisition.

In the end, the PEG did make two acquisitions from the group of 80 companies. Then they turned around and built their management teams by targeting the other 78 companies for their best managers. They hired away senior talent, including a chief operating officer, a chief technology officer, and a vice president of sales, among many others.

The PEG had used the veil of an acquisition to go on a fishing trip for managers, and the owners of these businesses had been duped into revealing too much, too early.

THE DANGER OF A PROPRIETARY DEAL

The opposite of a slow information reveal is a proprietary deal, where an acquirer takes control of the entire process and you're left revealing everything about your business much too early in the process.[16]

Acquirers land a proprietary deal (or "prop deal") when they convince you to enter into a negotiation to sell your business to them without creating a marketplace for it. Acquirers running a proprietary deal recognize that they do not have competition, and they tend to make weaker offers with more punitive terms because they know nobody else is bidding.

Possibly worse, when an acquirer knows they are the only potential purchaser interested in your business, they tend to drag out the process of evaluating your company and verifying what you tell them. This due diligence can last for many months in a proprietary deal, often resulting in the acquirer reducing their price at the end because they know you are exhausted by the process and have no other buyer to turn to.

Many founders become the target of a proprietary deal without even knowing they have been tricked. It can happen so easily. Someone senior from the acquiring company approaches you, complimenting you on your business. The acquirer suggests a meeting at a fancy restaurant. You agree, figuring, what could be the harm?

The danger is, you're about to lose control of your dance.

Before we go any further, let's take a minute to think about the background of the guy or gal you're about to dine with. Chances are, if your potential acquirer is an individual investor, that person is sophisticated enough to have reached a position in life to have (or

---

16   Also may be referred to as a "negotiated sale."

be able to borrow) the money to buy your business, so probably is a reasonably savvy negotiator.

If you're approached instead by a partner in a PEG, remember that they are among the most experienced businesspeople on the planet. Such people almost always have a business degree, very often come from a career in your industry, and make their living buying and selling companies.

If your suitor is a big company, they will likely dispatch a division president who presides over thousands of employees or a head of corporate development. Here again, these individuals are among the most erudite dealmakers on earth. They spend most of their life negotiating, whether it is building a global partnership, extracting themselves from an employee dispute, or buying a company.

Regardless of who courts you in a proprietary deal, expect them to be smooth. They will be easy to talk to and liberal with their praise of the company you have built. They may offer wine and work to slowly lower your defenses. They will try to make you believe they are your friend.

Don't believe them.

ASKING "WHAT" QUESTIONS

At some point in their courting of you, potential buyers will subtly start to ask questions about your business that you may not be in the habit of revealing over dinner—confidential stuff like your revenue, gross margin, and profitability. These are your privates, and you may not want to reveal them just yet.

I'm not saying you should never go to lunch with an industry colleague. But whenever you draw the attention of another company that dispatches someone senior (or anyone with a title that includes the words "corporate development" or "business development"), assume they are fishing for a potential acquisition, and make sure you don't reveal something you will end up regretting. There will be a time to share this private information—just not yet.

In advance of a meeting with an industry peer, develop your list of "what" questions. Questions that begin with the word "what" are open-ended inquiries that will get someone talking—and avoid you having to carry the conversation and risk revealing too much. For example, take control of the conversation by asking your suitor questions like:

- What do you see as the biggest trends likely to impact our industry in the future?
- What drives your business model?
- What attributes do you look for in a partner?
- What do you see as the synergies between our companies?

How Dan Martell Avoided a Proprietary Deal When Selling Clarity.fm

Savvy sellers avoid the proprietary deal by creating a competitive process for acquiring their company. Take, for example, Dan Martell—the founder of Clarity.fm, among other companies. When

Martell decided to sell Clarity,[17] he knew the likely buyer was one of three New York–based companies. Instead of negotiating with just one, he invited all three to an event he hosted in New York. The three CEOs—all of whom knew one another—saw a room full of their competitors and realized that if Clarity went on the market, they would have to outbid the other buyers in that room.

Hosting the event was Martell's way of artfully communicating to all the potential buyers that a proprietary deal was off the table and that if they wanted to buy Clarity, they would have to compete for it.

TAKING ACTION

It's flattering to receive a call from an executive at a company you respect. Just know that if you accept their invitation to lunch, you run the risk of becoming the latest casualty of the proprietary deal.

Aim to talk less than 10% of the time, and don't reveal any of your numbers just yet. Remember, the art of selling your business well is to control the striptease—revealing information slowly and intentionally to heighten the desire of all would-be suitors.

The chapters that follow will give you a system for ensuring you divulge the right information at the right point in the process. In the meantime, go ahead and accept a free lunch from an industry peer or a partner in a PEG. But go alone, and let them do all the talking.

---

17 John Warrillow, "Negotiation Secrets from Three Exits," *Built to Sell Radio*, podcast, August 30, 2017, https://builttosell.com/radio/episode-107/

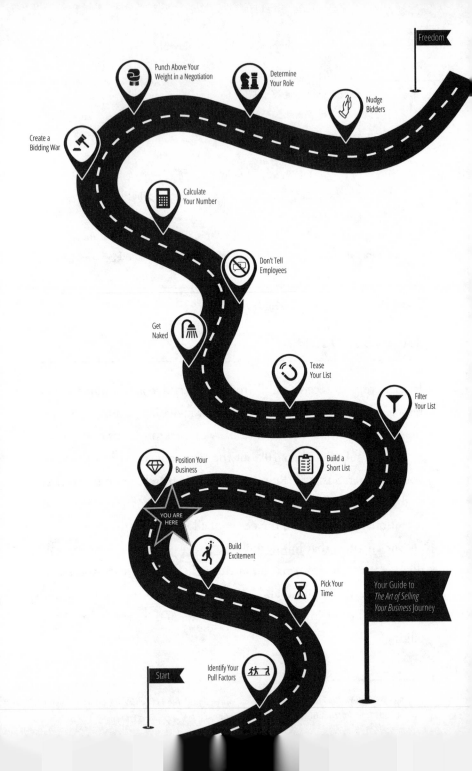

Freedom

Punch Above Your Weight in a Negotiation

Determine Your Role

Nudge Bidders

Create a Bidding War

Calculate Your Number

Don't Tell Employees

Get Naked

Tease Your List

Filter Your List

Position Your Business

Build a Short List

YOU ARE HERE

Build Excitement

Pick Your Time

Your Guide to *The Art of Selling Your Business* Journey

Start

Identify Your Pull Factors

Chapter 5

FISH WHERE
THEY ARE BITING

HOW TO POSITION YOUR
COMPANY TO BE ACQUIRED

My epiphany about the role of an entrepreneur almost never happened.

Along with 60 other business owners, I was attending a three-year program on the executive education campus at MIT. The program—led by Verne Harnish, the legendary founder of Entrepreneurs' Organization, or EO—had the pretentious name Birthing of Giants.[18] It featured a group of ambitious entrepreneurs conven-

---

18   Birthing of Giants has since been rebranded by its owner, Entrepreneurs' Organization, as the Entrepreneurial Masters Program, or EMP.

ing at MIT for one week a year. We had been selected from a pool of applicants who all met the same criteria: own a growing company with at least $1 million in annual sales and be under the age of 40.

In the first year, we heard from the legendary Jack Stack on the benefits of employee ownership. The next year, Patrick Lencioni, the author of *The Five Dysfunctions of a Team* and many other best-sellers, spoke about leadership. In the final year of the program, Stephen Watkins, an entrepreneur who had recently sold his business, spoke to us.

I was going to skip Watkins's session. I had never heard of him and had tired of the trite, rags-to-riches success story of the cashed-out entrepreneur. However, my classmates were all going, so I decided to suspend my skepticism and join in.

I'm glad I did.

Watkins began by canvassing the room to see how many of us were personally involved in selling our company's product or service to our customers. I, along with nearly every other entrepreneur in the room, raised my hand.

With that, he proceeded to scold us all for spending too much time selling our products and virtually no time selling our company. He went further, and I'll try to paraphrase his message for you: "Your job as an entrepreneur is to hire salespeople to sell your products and services so you can spend your time selling and marketing your company. You make a few hundred or a few thousand dollars when you sell your product, but if you turned those same skills to selling your *company*, you can make exponentially more. You have the right skills, but you're selling the wrong product."

He paused, took a long pull from a bottle of water, and let his message sink in.

Watkins then explained that entrepreneurs add the most value when they design and start their business; the return on their time invested starts to go down rapidly as the business gets going. The entrepreneurs who earn the best return on their investment of money, time, and energy are the ones who get in and out quickly.

Watkins's message landed on me with blunt force. I felt like an amateur who had gotten a glimpse at a professional game and realized the pros were playing with an entirely different set of rules. Here I was, spinning my wheels while selling my company's services, when I should have been marketing my company to potential acquirers.

From that day forward, the way I thought about my role changed. I started hiring salespeople to call on customers. At first, I missed the adrenaline rush of personally making a big sale, but in time, I came to enjoy seeing other people land big customers even more.

I still went out on sales calls, but they were to people I thought might one day buy my *company*, not my product.

You've spent years marketing your products and services, and now it is time to apply everything you know about marketing and selling to your most important product of all: your company.

POSITIONING: THE FOUNDATION ON WHICH ALL GREAT MARKETING RESTS

Every great marketing campaign—whether it's a product or a company—begins with positioning what you have to offer in the mind of the consumer.

Positioning is a concept that was first popularized by advertising legends Al Ries and Jack Trout in a series of articles they wrote for the trade magazine *Advertising Age* (now the global media company Ad Age) back in 1972. Their articles went on to become a book called *Positioning: The Battle for Your Mind*, which is arguably the best book ever written on the marketing principle of positioning. It still holds up today and is well worth reading.

All the way back in 1972, Ries and Trout argued that consumers are bombarded by advertising messages. If the authors thought it was bad back then, they should try living in today's hyperconnected world where the battle for our mind has turned into a bare-knuckle, winner-takes-all cage match for our notification-swamped brain.

What happens when your mind reaches the point of saturation and you can't absorb any more information? You look for shortcuts. In other words, you find ways to quickly categorize information into buckets you've already formed in your mind. It's the only way to keep up.

Trying to create a new bucket in someone's mind is virtually impossible. That's why, Ries and Trout argued, the best marketers take what is already in the mind of the consumer and attach their product or service to these existing neural pathways.

"The basic approach of positioning," Ries and Trout opined, "is not to create something new and different, but to manipulate what's already up there in the mind, to retie the connections that already exist."[19]

Ries and Trout used the introduction of Miller Lite™ as an example. The marketers behind the launch of Miller Lite knew consumers already have a well-formed groove in their mind around what beer is. When we hear the word "beer," we don't need someone to explain it to us. If you're anything like me, the moment you see the word "beer" on the page, your mind conjures the rich-tasting nectar served cold in a frosty glass.

That's why Miller's positioning line for the introduction of Miller Lite was so perfect: "Everything you've always wanted in a beer. And less." They were taking the information already in our mind about beer and introducing a slight twist.

The brain doesn't have to work hard to put a message like this in its rightful place. Positioning starts with inserting your message inside an existing bucket within the mind of your prospect and then offering a simple point of differentiation to set it slightly apart from everything else inside the bucket.

ACQUIRERS RELY ON BUCKETS TOO

Acquirers are just like consumers. They are drowning in messages and rely on shortcuts to process it all.

They already have preexisting ideas of the kinds of companies they want to buy. Your job is to position your business as something unique in a category they're already interested in.

---

19 Al Ries and Jack Trout, *Positioning: The Battle for Your Mind* (New York: McGraw-Hill, 1986).

This may sound devious, but it's not. Positioning is one of the reasons selling your business is more art than science. Anyone can blandly recount your financial achievements and get an average acquisition offer, but your goal is to do better than average. That comes down to the narrative you weave about your business—and it all starts with how you position what you've built and what it can do for a buyer.

As Ries and Trout point out, this is not about changing your company. It's about changing the way acquirers *perceive* your company—and making sure they put it in the right bucket.

How you position your company has always mattered to your customers, but now that you're thinking of selling, it also matters to potential acquirers. The trick is to understand the kind of company that is selling in your industry and to make sure you look like one of those to a buyer.

Let's imagine you have an alternative energy company that installs solar panels, geothermal heating, and windmills. Further, you come to learn that PEGs are snatching up solar energy companies.

You have a choice to make. Option A is to position your company as an alternative energy business that installs all sorts of green energy systems, but this risks being overlooked by the private equity community that is looking to acquire solar companies specifically. A PEG will be comparing your business to hundreds of other potential acquisition candidates and may just pass right by you.

Option B is to position your company as a leader in solar energy that, as part of your commitment to alternative energy solutions like solar, also offers wind and geothermal solutions where solar energy is not practical.

Which option is more likely to catch the attention of a PEG looking to invest in solar companies? Option B—where the company is clearly positioned as a solar company first rather than as a diversified alternative energy company.

Acquirers are busy and may spend only a few minutes evaluating your business before they decide to pass or dig in. Although positioning your business well is not likely to be enough to garner an offer, it may be enough to get an acquirer to invest a little more time to understand what makes your business unique.

WHAT HAPPENS WHEN YOU FALL INTO THE WRONG BUCKET?

For an example of how positioning can impact the value of your business, let's look at Jeffrey Feldberg, Waleuska Lazo, and Stephen Wells, who found themselves in the wrong bucket in the minds of acquirers when they received their first unsolicited offer to sell Embanet.[20] The partners co-founded Embanet in 1995 to help prestigious colleges like Vanderbilt and Boston University deliver online degree programs.

In the beginning, Embanet was a classic service business. A few years after starting, they were approached by an acquirer who offered them around three times profit for their business. Twenty-four months later, the founders said "yes" to a nine-figure offer based on 13 times EBITDA.

What happened? How did Embanet go from being worth 3

---

20   John Warrillow, "3 x EBITDA to 13 x EBITDA in Just 2.5 Years," *Built to Sell Radio*, podcast, April 4, 2018, https://builttosell.com/radio/episode-133/

times earnings to 13 times without changing the core of what they did? Part of the transformation was a change in how the partners *positioned* Embanet in the eyes of an acquirer.

Embanet's first acquisition offer of three times earnings is pretty typical for a small professional services firm where the assets—as the old saying goes—"go up and down the elevator every night." The acquirer was looking at Embanet as a simple website development agency that happened to focus on colleges. The acquirer likely had a box in their mind for what small web design businesses were worth and simply offered the going rate.

The second acquirer knew that every institution of higher learning was trying to figure out how to increase their reach through instructor-led online courses and knew Embanet was a market leader. The first acquirer had seen Embanet as a simple website business, where the second saw a juggernaut in the e-learning industry.

TAKING ACTION

When an acquirer makes the decision to buy a company in a specific industry, the first thing they will likely do is perform an online search for the industry's leading companies. Review your website, and ensure that it clearly positions you as a leader in the industry where companies are looking to make acquisitions. Then invest in SEO so you will naturally rank among the leading companies in that industry.

Also, consider becoming a more active member of your industry. If your sector gives out awards, toss your name in the ring. If your industry has a conference, volunteer to speak about something you do well. If your industry association has a board of directors, apply to become a member.

These actions will not only help new customers find you in the short term, but they will also position your company in the right bucket in the minds of acquirers when you're ready to sell.

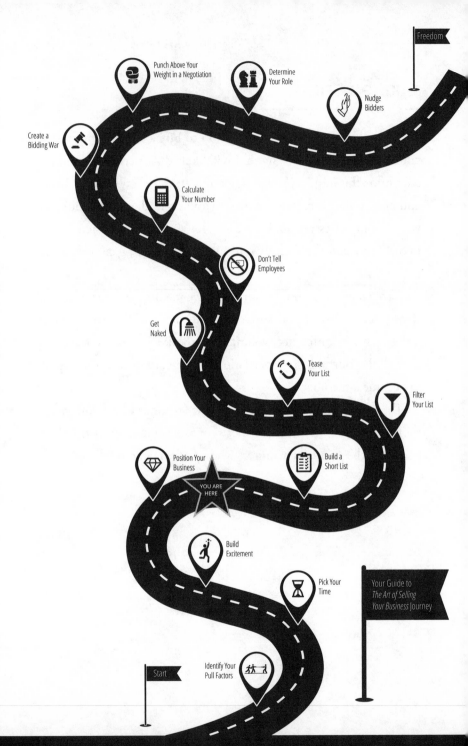

Freedom

Punch Above Your Weight in a Negotiation

Determine Your Role

Nudge Bidders

Create a Bidding War

Calculate Your Number

Don't Tell Employees

Get Naked

Tease Your List

Filter Your List

Position Your Business

YOU ARE HERE

Build a Short List

Build Excitement

Pick Your Time

Your Guide to *The Art of Selling Your Business* Journey

Start

Identify Your Pull Factors

This map is intended as a visual representation of the journey you'll take to sell your business. You can also download *The Art of Selling Your Business*

Chapter 6

PLAYING THE FIELD

UNDERSTANDING THE THREE
TYPES OF ACQUIRERS

David Chang was lost.

He had just returned home from his tour of duty in Iraq and needed to figure out what to do with his life.

Chang had a knack for numbers and had learned a lot about operations through his military training, so he decided to go into business with some friends. They started a home renovation company called CS Design Builders, which began by installing granite countertops and quickly expanded into a full-service home renovation company.

Chang helped build CS Design Builders up to a dozen employees and a little over $1 million in annual revenue when he decided it was time to sell. Chang hired a broker who found a buyer willing to offer $1 million cash for CS Design Builders. Chang was thrilled, but as the transaction marched toward a close, the buyer asked to restructure the deal.

The acquirer proposed to raise his acquisition offer to $1.2 million—with a catch. Under the terms of the new deal, Chang would now get just 20% of his sale proceeds up front, and the rest would be paid in monthly installments over a few years. The agreement included a provision that if the buyer ever missed a payment, Chang would get his business back.

Chang preferred the sound of the all-cash deal, but since that was no longer an offer and he was keen to move on with his life, he agreed to finance the new owner.

It didn't take long before Chang realized he had made a mistake.

The new owners missed their first payment, then their second. In the meantime, Chang heard that his former employees had started to leave the company. He also began fielding calls from his former suppliers who hadn't been paid.

Back when Chang had started CS Design Builders, he'd signed personal guarantees with his bank and some key suppliers. What he hadn't realized at the time of sale was that even though he had sold the assets of his business, he was still personally liable for the outstanding debt he had incurred while operating it.

Chang ended up taking his business back, but it was not much more than a shell of its former self. Most of the employees had left, business had dried up, and suppliers were hounding Chang for their money. Defeated, Chang shut the business down and worked out a payment plan with his suppliers to settle his many debts.

David Chang's story is a cautionary tale of what can happen when you sell your business to an unprepared buyer. Individual investors are one of three types of acquirers, all of which offer positive and negative aspects. This chapter provides a brief look at the most common types of business acquirers, their typical motivations, and the pros and cons of selling to each.

Rather than close your mind to one type or another, remain open to all of these options to maximize the odds that you can create competition for your business.

Acquirer Type 1: Individual Investor

If your business is on the smaller side—less than a few million dollars in annual revenue—it might be intriguing to an individual looking for an investment or seeking to replace a job they have recently lost or left. People who are downsized or who leave a company midcareer often bristle at the idea of going back to work for someone again and therefore look at acquiring a business as a way to be their own boss. They are usually somewhat established financially and have some experience, so if your business is relatively small and consistently profitable, an individual may be able to borrow the money to buy it.

Individual investors are generally less sophisticated than strategic acquirers or financial buyers (such as PEGs), which means you may be able to drive a better deal with less scrutiny over the details of your business than you might endure when selling to a strategic investor.

It's rare that an individual investor pays cash for an acquisition. Typically, in order to gather most of the money to buy your business, individual investors borrow from two places: a bank and you.

Instead of taking all of your proceeds in cash, when you agree to finance some of the sale, you offer to accept some of your money over time while the buyer uses your business as collateral for your loan. When it goes well, the buyer takes some of the profits from running your company and pays you back—often with interest. If the buyer fails to pay you, as in the case of David Chang from CS Design Builders, you are almost always second in line behind the bank, which will ensure they get paid before you see any of your money.

The art of negotiating with an individual investor

Along with typically being less sophisticated buyers, individual investors are also usually the least well financed. In some countries, the government will guarantee a bank loan to an individual investor to buy a business (e.g., an SBA loan in the United States), provided the deal meets a set of criteria. Make sure you understand what makes an individual eligible for a government-backed loan to buy your business.

Some individual investors are trying entrepreneurship for the first time, so they might end up being hopeless at actually running your business. Others may fail when they try to graft their big business strategies onto a company like yours. Running a small business is less strategy and more street fight, and if the buyer doesn't get that, they will struggle with the messy work of actually running something.

Therefore, strive to get as much cash up front as you can, and be clear on what you're willing to do to help the new buyer learn your business. Plan to stay involved for a while to show them the ropes.

Aim for a deal where you consider the portion of your proceeds from a sale that are being paid overtime as "gravy," so if the buyer fails, you're still satisfied with the transaction.

Remember, your goal at this point in the process should be to maximize the number of offers you receive (and by extension, your negotiating leverage) by remaining open to all types of potential acquirers.

ACQUIRER TYPE 2: PRIVATE EQUITY GROUP

Another possible acquirer for your business is a PEG. This category can be further divided into three types:

1. A fund, usually with multiple shareholders, that is set up to buy, improve, and flip companies (typically within five to seven years).

2. A family office that is interested in investing money in a sector, usually on behalf of a wealthy family (or families), and often with no immediate plans to sell.

3. A fundless sponsor—an individual or individuals who think they can raise the money to buy a business. This is usually someone who wants to own a business, thinks they can add value by operating it better than it's being run today, and has contacts willing to financially back them if the terms are favorable enough.

There was a time when PEGs considered investing only in companies with a few million dollars of EBITDA. But as more money has flowed into private equity, acquirers have gone "down market," and now some consider buying companies with less than $1 million in annual profit if those companies meet their other investment criteria.

PEGs are generally run by people who have already sold a business or have gone to a fancy business school. Their game is to find a business that is scalable or, in their view, is underperforming and could benefit from additional capital and more sophisticated management.

The idea is usually to bring some business school rigor to running your company, maximize its value, and turn around and sell it for much more than they paid (or occasionally, as is the case with many family offices, keep it to spit out cash for the long run).

One of the tricks PEGs use is to apply a lot of debt to maximize their return. Similar to buying a house with a small deposit, the leverage allows the buyer to amplify their returns for shareholders if things go as planned.[21] To borrow money using your business as collateral, your business has to be what industry insiders call "bankable," meaning it is a business that consistently generates profits that would allow a bank loan to be paid back with some wiggle room if things go south. That's why PEGs are usually looking for larger, more mature businesses that have a consistent track record of making money.

You may be asking, "Why would a bigger business with consistent profits want to sell to one of these guys?" The answer often

---

21   Debt also amplifies investment losses and can make it hard for your business to grow, because you have to use available cash to pay down debt rather than invest in the business to grow.

comes down to the way a PEG structures their acquisitions. Unless it's a fundless sponsor, PEGs typically don't have managers to run a business like yours, so they may ask you to stick around by offering you a "second bite of the apple." This is a term used to describe an acquisition model, which involves you keeping some of your equity and continuing to play a leadership role in your business after the PEG invests.

PEGs usually acquire the first part of a company for a relatively low valuation. Their pitch—very common with a private equity fund—is that the second part of your equity will be sold for a higher multiple because their management practices and the synergies with their other investments will make your business much more valuable than it is under your leadership. This arrangement is often attractive to owners who are not ready to retire. You get to sell part of your business, pay off your mortgage, and buy a few toys while continuing to hold an equity stake in a business that could be worth a lot more down the road.

In many cases, selling to a PEG works out just fine. In others, the former owner bristles under the yoke of their new boss.

Without all the synergies available to a strategic acquirer (discussed in the next section), the PEG has fewer levers to pull in order to make your business a lot more valuable after they invest. For example, PEGs use a lot of debt. This means your business will have to take its profits and pay down debt as its first priority. You may want to invest in a new marketing program or buy a new piece of machinery, but in a highly leveraged business, paying back the bank needs to happen ahead of anything else.

The other lever a PEG has for making your business more valuable is to overrule your decisions and "professionalize" your company. This is code for taking the policies and procedures you've created over the years and scrapping them for something more in line with industry standards.

This may sound reasonable in theory, but since you're likely the author of those policies, you may not like their choices. Your decisions may look amateurish to someone who spends their days in a boardroom, but a business is a delicate alchemy of give-and-take, and if a PEG doesn't understand the nuances of your company's culture, they may upset that balance.

WHAT HAPPENED WHEN LETTERLOGIC SOLD TO A PEG

As vice president of sales at IXT Solutions, Sherry Deutschmann thought she had some clout with her boss, but when she suggested ways to improve customer retention by increasing morale within the company, she was told she knew nothing about business.

So Deutschmann quit. She vowed to start her own company and compete with IXT in the business of printing and mailing patient statements for hospitals.

In January 2002, LetterLogic was born.

A single mother, Deutschmann didn't have much capital, so she held a yard sale to generate some cash. In an effort to be frugal, she even fashioned a desk for her new business out of an old door. It was a Spartan existence, but Deutschmann was able to sign up her first hospital by offering a money-back guarantee on returned mail—an offer the hospital found compelling, given the importance of the statements they were sending.

Deutschmann started hiring staff and making good on her promise to do things differently from how her former boss had done them. She began by gathering her small team in a make-shift boardroom every month to share the company's financials. In the months when they had made a profit, Deutschmann shared 10% of the money with her employees. She divided the profit-sharing proceeds equally among her staff, reasoning that each was equivalently important to the company's success.

In the early days, the profit-sharing proceeds amounted to only a few dollars per month, but Deutschmann persevered, knowing it was important that everyone feel they were part of the company's growth. The business continued to expand, and by 2016, LetterLogic was generating more than $40 million in annual sales, with profit margins approaching 10%.

The monthly profit-sharing checks had become real and, in some months, amounted to hundreds of dollars per employee—a lot of money for the hourly workers Deutschmann had on payroll.

The business continued to expand, but Deutschmann was conflicted. She had recently taken over as the primary caregiver of her granddaughter and knew she needed to be home more. Deutschmann decided it was time to sell. She hired an intermediary, who quickly received seven offers for LetterLogic.

The highest offer came from a PEG that claimed to be impressed with the transparent and empathetic culture Deutschmann had created. Said Deutschmann, "I felt like they were the most likely to maintain the culture and take care of the people the way I was used to taking care of them."[22] Feeling like the PEG was going

---

22 John Warrillow, "The Snag of Selling to Private Equity," *Built to Sell Radio*, podcast, November 8, 2019, https://builttosell.com/radio/episode-205/

to honor her legacy, Deutschmann accepted their offer of more than seven times EBITDA.

It was the biggest payday of her life—and Deutschmann decided to share the proceeds with her employees. She took 15% of the money and divided it among her staff based on their tenure. The week after selling, Deutschmann called each employee into her office and personally handed them a check, which amounted to tens of thousands of dollars in many cases. One young woman took the cash and paid off her parents' mortgage.

For Deutschmann, it was a high point that would quickly be followed by an equally emotional low point when the PEG immediately ended LetterLogic's profit sharing plan.

Having agreed to stay on as a board member, she couldn't bear to watch the new owner dismantle the culture she had painstakingly created. "It was just too painful to watch the changes they were making to the company," she said. Six months after selling to the PEG, Deutschmann resigned her seat on the board and left for good.

When I interviewed Deutschmann three years later, only 12 of her 51 employees had remained with the company.

The art of negotiating with a private equity group

Acquisition offers—regardless of whom they are from—give you leverage when negotiating, so don't turn your nose up at being acquired by a PEG. At the very least, you can use their offer as leverage.

A PEG is in the business of buying low and selling high. To be successful, they have to acquire profitable companies for as little money as possible and use a lot of debt in the process. For their strategy to work, they need to sell your business at a much higher multiple within a few years, so push hard to understand what they plan to do to make your business more valuable.

Most PEGs have similar investment criteria. They usually look for businesses that consistently generate profits from a protected niche with good managers in place. Chances are, if you're attractive to one PEG, you'll be attractive to lots of them, so play one off the other to squeeze them for the best price and deal terms—and to be sure of the right cultural fit.

ACQUIRER TYPE 3: STRATEGIC ACQUIRER

A strategic acquirer (or simply "a strategic" in M&A parlance) is a company with assets that become more valuable if they own your business. When considering the right buyer for you, ask yourself: Is there a company in your industry that could compete more effectively if they acquired your company?

Your business may be strategically valuable to another for a lot of reasons, but here are some of the most common things that owning your company will allow a strategic to do:

- Win more business from their competitors
- Differentiate their offering
- Enter a new market
- Capture more market share, and therefore raise prices and be more profitable

- Improve profit margins by spreading their overhead across more revenue

You may find strategic acquirers will offer a higher price for your business than the other two types, because they can see a quick return on their investment from the synergies that come from owning your business.

How does a strategic acquisition differ from a private equity deal? By way of an example, let's look at Home Depot's acquisition of Blinds.com.[23]

Blinds.com was started by Jay Steinfeld, who studied accounting at the University of Texas and was hired by KPMG after college. He went on to become vice president of finance at Meineke Car Care Centers, Inc., the nationwide automotive franchisor.

Steinfeld left Meineke in 1985. Midcareer and out of work, he joined his wife's business, selling blinds in her retail store. Her business was such a success, he decided to open a second store to run himself.

Steinfeld quickly discovered that life as a retailer was harder than he'd imagined. He worked in the store six days a week and did the books at home on Sundays. Many nights, he didn't get home until after nine o'clock. Determined to find a better way, Steinfeld began researching the emerging field of selling online. It was 1993.

---

23 John Warrillow, "Lessons from Home Depot's Acquisition of a $100 Million Juggernaut Blinds.com," *Built to Sell Radio*, podcast, September 6, 2017, https://builttosell.com/radio/episode-108/

Steinfeld invested $1,500 in his first online website, which was essentially an electronic version of his brochure.

Over the next few years, Steinfeld continued to experiment with online advertising. His business model was crude. When customers responded to an ad, Steinfeld instructed his staff to tell the caller that someone from the customer service department would call them right back. The employee in the store would then call Steinfeld—who in those days spent most of his time driving around Houston selling blinds to people in their homes—to let him know someone had responded to his ad. Steinfeld would pull off to the side of the road and call the customer back. With calculator and notepad in hand, he would take their order from the front seat of his minivan.

By 1994, while Steinfeld was tooling around Houston in his van, Jeff Bezos was experimenting with selling books online. Amazon's early success got Steinfeld wondering whether people would buy blinds online. He ran the idea by a few customers, who balked, saying that blinds were different from books because they needed to be measured and installed. Undeterred, Steinfeld invested $3,000 to build his first online store.

He continued to tweak his approach to advertising and selling blinds online. Eventually, Steinfeld got to the point where his online orders eclipsed the $1.5 million in annual sales he was making through the store. In 2001, Steinfeld decided to go 100% online and launched Blinds.com.

By the end of 2013, Blinds.com had grown to 175 employees and, at more than $100 million in yearly revenue, was the largest online retailer of blinds in America. Even though Home Depot had close to $90 billion in annual sales at the time, Blinds.com was outperforming them in this tiny niche, which made the online company absolutely irresistible to the retail giant.

On January 23, 2014, Home Depot announced the acquisition of Blinds.com.[24] Home Depot's CEO at the time, Frank Blake, described their strategic rationale thus: "The acquisition of Blinds.com positions us well for expansion in the quickly growing online window coverings market. In addition, their unique sales and service model is one we hope to learn from as we continue to create even better interconnected retail experiences for our customers."[25]

My personal interpretation of Blake's comments (although I have no inside knowledge of Home Depot's strategy) is that, along with wanting to dominate a growing product category, Home Depot was keen to figure out how they could grow their online sales of other products customers traditionally only felt comfortable buying in a store.

Let's imagine Home Depot could leverage what they learned from Blinds.com and apply that insight to all of their product categories for a 1% improvement in overall sales. On a $90 billion base of revenue, that 1% lift is worth $900 million in incremental sales per year to Home Depot. So you can see how they saw Blinds.com as a strategic acquisition.

---

24 John Warrillow, "Lessons from Home Depot's Acquisition of a $100 Million Juggernaut Blinds.com," *Built to Sell Radio*, podcast, September 6, 2017, https://builttosell.com/radio/episode-108/

25 HomeDepot.com, "The Home Depot Acquires Blinds.com," press release, January 23, 2014, https://ir.homedepot.com/news-releases/2014/01-23-2014-014522229

The art of negotiating with a strategic acquirer

The strategic acquirer is not a person; it's a thing. It's an organization run by a CEO who reports to a board with the primary responsibility of maximizing value for their shareholders. Unlike other acquirers, a strategic acquirer is—and always will be—in love with *their* company.

Thinking a strategic acquirer will help you reach your goals through their resources is the wrong way to approach them. The strategic acquirer is focused on their business, products, and people. Although you may care deeply about your company, they don't feel the same and likely never will. Instead, they want to know how owning your business will help make theirs more successful.

THE HYBRID PRIVATE EQUITY GROUP

There is actually a fourth kind of acquirer: a mash-up of a traditional PEG and a strategic acquirer. These hybrid PEGs specialize in buying companies in a specific industry, which means you could make a case they are actually a hybrid.

An acquaintance of mine, for example, is a partner in one hybrid PEG that is buying up small dental practices. This PEG's objective is to buy small offices, roll them together, and take advantage of additional buying power for the supplies dentists need. The long-term goal is to sell the group down the road for a lot more than they paid for the individual parts. Technically they are a PEG, but in practice, they are acting more like a strategic acquirer.

TAKING ACTION

Continue to keep your mind open to the idea of being acquired by any one of a range of buyers.

Many potential acquirers will need to borrow money to buy your business. A bank will want to understand how they will be paid back, so they will review your company's ability to churn out cash. Therefore, ensure your business shows consistent (or growing) profits on your tax return for at least three years leading up to a sale.

Offer something unique that customers love and competitors find difficult to match, and you may also be attractive to a strategic acquirer.

The more appealing you are to a range of buyers, the more likely you are to draw multiple offers, which is the secret to maximizing your company's value in a negotiation.

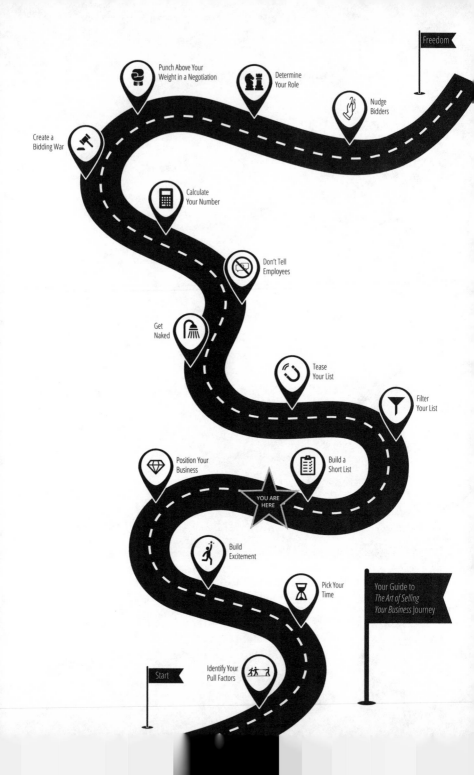

Freedom

Punch Above Your Weight in a Negotiation

Determine Your Role

Nudge Bidders

Create a Bidding War

Calculate Your Number

Don't Tell Employees

Get Naked

Tease Your List

Filter Your List

Position Your Business

Build a Short List

YOU ARE HERE

Build Excitement

Pick Your Time

Your Guide to
*The Art of Selling
Your Business* Journey

Start

Identify Your Pull Factors

Chapter 7

BUILDING YOUR LIST

HOW TO IDENTIFY A
POTENTIAL ACQUIRER

Now that you know the range of potential acquirers, it's time to develop a long list of candidates who might buy your business. We need to go from theorizing about buyer types to writing actual company names on a list of possible acquirers, which is something Peter Kelly knows all about.

Kelly came to the United States from Ireland to earn an MBA at Stanford. As his graduation in the spring of 1999 neared, Kelly couldn't help but notice how many industries were being transformed through the proliferation of the internet.

Kelly observed that while consumers were getting more comfortable searching for used cars online, car dealers were still relying on physical auctions to purchase their used car inventory. Dealers would attend auctions with used cars rolling by on massive conveyor belts, leaving the dealer just seconds to assess each prospective car.

Sensing an opportunity, Kelly started OPENLANE to disrupt the old-school way of selling used cars to dealers. OPENLANE offered them the opportunity to shop for used car inventory on a private website just for wholesalers, where they could take their time to assess each car individually.

Over the next decade, Kelly grew OPENLANE to more than 300 employees and $100 million in annual sales. Along the way, he met with a handful of potential acquirers, including the traditional auctioneers Kelly was displacing with his online marketplace.

By 2011, business was strong, but Kelly always felt his success was somewhat precarious. A number of car manufacturers had created their own online marketplaces, and some existing industry players had developed their own competitive offerings in response.

Sensing his luck might run out, Kelly decided to sell OPENLANE. Because he didn't want the word to get out among the car manufacturers, he contacted just three strategic acquirers that had approached him in the past. He felt confident he could create some competitive tension among them, because all three had approached him in the past about an acquisition. In the end, Kelly got two offers and sold OPEN-LANE for almost $250 million to KAR Auction Services, one of the physical auctioneers he had been disrupting for more than a decade.[26]

---

26   John Warrillow, "Deciding When to Sell," *Built to Sell Radio*, podcast, September 20, 2019, https://builttosell.com/radio/episode-199/

Like positioning (which we discussed in chapter 5), deciding whom to approach about buying your business is more art than science. In Kelly's case, he was comfortable limiting the list to a handful of strategic acquirers, because all three had already expressed interest in buying OPENLANE. In your case, you may need a considerably longer list.

CHOOSE THE BEST TYPE OF AUCTION FOR YOU

Your ultimate goal is to attract a handful of offers so that you can play one off the other to ensure you're getting the best price going for a business like yours. You may choose to list a small business (for example, one worth less than $1 million) on the open market, while a larger company is likely best served by developing a long list of potential acquirers and approaching them directly.

The length of your list depends on how big your company is and how important confidentiality is in your industry. Clearly, a longer list increases the odds that you'll be able to drum up multiple offers, but the more buyers you approach, the higher the chances word will get out that you are trying to sell. Although you'll ask every potential acquirer to sign an NDA, the news that you're selling still has a funny way of trickling out through the industry.

As you contemplate the number of potential acquirers you will select for your list, consider the pros and cons to the following approaches.

Broad auction

In a broad auction, you may approach up to 100 potential acquirers—or even more. Casting the net this wide is designed to maximize your odds of getting multiple offers and being able to drive the highest possible price.

The downsides of a broad auction are that it can be difficult to maintain confidentiality and is the most time-consuming and disruptive approach. You may also turn off some potential acquirers who refuse to participate in a broad auction on principle, for fear of being used as a pawn in an attempt to lever up value. Others may hesitate to purchase a company whose secrets have been laid bare for the entire industry to see.

Limited auction

In a limited auction, you target anywhere from 10 to 50 potential acquirers. A limited auction is usually sufficient to create multiple offers, but it can still be disruptive in the ways described just above.

Targeted auction

In a targeted auction, you handpick a half dozen or so companies you are confident will want to make you an offer.

A targeted auction is usually used when selling a very large company (i.e., revenues of $500 million and up) where the universe of potential buyers is quite small or the consequences of a breach in confidentiality are severe.

A targeted auction is less disruptive and easier to keep confidential when compared with a broader auction. The downside is that you may overestimate the demand for your business and go through the process without getting an offer. Companies on your targeted list will all have their own priorities and financial restrictions. As an outsider, you have no way of knowing whether buying you out is a possibility.

Targeted auctions are usually used for situations like OPEN-LANE, where confidentially is critical, the universe of buyers is small, and you can be reasonably sure each will be interested in making an offer.

Proprietary deal

An exclusive negotiation with one buyer means you have little negotiating leverage and lose much of the control over the process of selling, as we covered in chapter 4. It's also rare to maximize your value with just one bidder, so you'll likely leave money on the table. For an acquirer that knows there is nobody else bidding, it is common to delay due diligence and lower their original offer after their investigation is complete.

Although the cons of a proprietary deal usually outweigh the pros, there are some benefits of a negotiated sale with one buyer—namely, that you maximize the chance of keeping your deal confidential, and that having one bidder is generally the least disruptive for you and your team. Occasionally, a proprietary deal can make sense when you are in an industry that trades in a narrow range and you are being preemptively offered a price at the top end of the established range of multiples.

STOCK YOUR LIST WITH STRATEGIC ACQUIRERS

As you develop your long list of potential acquirers, focus on strategic buyers who usually have the capacity (and, hopefully, the willingness) to pay more for your business. As we saw in the case of KAR's acquisition of OPENLANE, a strategic acquirer is usually a larger company somewhere in your industry. They may be a direct competitor, an indirect rival, or just another company in your sector.

A strategic acquirer is evaluating your business based on what it is worth *in their hands*. They will try to estimate how much more of their product or service they can sell if they add you into the mix. Because of their size, this can often lead to buyers who are willing and able to pay much more for your business.

For example, Tom Franceski and his two partners had built their content management firm, DocStar, up to 45 employees when they decided to shop the business to some PEGs.[27] The PEGs offered between four and six times EBITDA, which Franceski deemed low for a fast-growing software company.

Franceski was then approached by a strategic acquirer called Epicor, which is a global software business with a lot of customers that could use what DocStar had built. Epicor offered DocStar a multiple of *revenue*—a much fatter multiple than the modest multiple of profit the PEGs were offering.

---

27 John Warrillow, "The Strategic vs. The Financial Buyer," *Built to Sell Radio*, podcast, October 4, 2017, https://builttosell.com/radio/episode-111/

WHEN PARTNERS BECOME ACQUIRERS

As you contemplate your long list, remember that strategic acquirers are usually already in your industry—and your most natural acquirer may even be an existing partner or investor. Cultivating relationships with the natural strategic acquirers in your sector is smart business strategy—which is something Steve Murch knew from the earliest days of his travel company, VacationSpot.com.

The travel industry has gone through two major evolutions in the past 30 years. Our parents booked travel through an agent, but in the 1990s, websites like Expedia or Hotels.com became the standard. The second major transformation in the travel industry was led by Murch.

In 1997, Murch was a Seattle-based software engineer leading the Internet Games Group at Microsoft when he noticed a gap in the travel market. It was easy to use Expedia to book a hotel, but if you were looking for a villa, chalet, or private condominium online, you were out of luck. Murch imagined a website where vacation homeowners could list their location with pictures and a description—where travelers looking to stay somewhere other than a hotel could search for a private home or condo to rent.

In 1997, more than a decade before Airbnb would accelerate the travel industry's second major transformation into the sharing economy, Murch launched VacationSpot.com to connect travelers with private vacation homes. As with any marketplace, Murch knew the key to his success would be solving the chicken-or-egg problem: travelers would use the site only if there was enough variety of homes available, and owners would list their property only if there was enough traffic.

Rather than giving up most of his equity in a series of costly fundraising rounds to get the money he would need to drive traffic, Murch approached Expedia with an idea. In return for exclusive access to Expedia's users who came to the site looking to book accommodations other than a traditional hotel, Murch would give them 20% of his company.

Unbeknownst to Expedia, Murch had an ulterior motive for partnering with them. He knew they would make an excellent strategic acquirer for his business one day—and they did. Three years later, Expedia bought VacationSpot.com for $87 million.[28]

WHY EVEN BOTHER WITH FINANCIAL BUYERS?

You may be asking, "Why bother even including PEGs and other financial buyers if strategic acquirers will pay so much more?" Here are three reasons to keep some financial buyers, including PEGs, on your list:

1. **You can use them as a pawn.** As I touched on earlier, to gin up your value, you want as many offers for your business as possible. While you may not want to sell to a financial acquirer, you can use them as a dispensable pawn for leverage in getting a better offer from a strategic buyer.

2. **Financial buyers also make strategic acquisitions.** Some financial buyers are actually strategic acquirers in disguise.

---

28   John Warrillow, "4 Big Exits, 1 Smart Entrepreneur," *Built to Sell Radio*, podcast, November 2, 2018, https://builttosell.com/radio/episode-158/

If a PEG is rolling up multiple companies in the same industry, they are actually a hybrid of sorts (as discussed in the previous chapter). Their structure may be that of a PEG, but with synergies to capture by owning more than one company in the same industry, they may act more like a strategic acquirer and be willing to offer you some of the strategic premium.

3. **Why not have your cake and eat it too?** PEGs usually want you to remain in your business for a few years after you sell it. So if you're not quite ready to leave your company, and you're willing to sell part of your business while continuing to hold some shares and stay on as CEO, a PEG might be the perfect buyer for your company.

TAKING ACTION

Start to develop a long list of companies that may have a strategic reason to buy your business. You need to learn as much as possible about each potential acquirer's business and imagine all the ways they could benefit from owning your company (M&A professionals refer to this as an "investment thesis"). For example, would owning your business give an acquirer:

- A point of differentiation for their marketing?

- A leg up in competing with their archrival?

- A big enough share of the market to control the price of a key product or service?

- Access to a new market?

- A way to save money?

- A new list of customers for their product?

- A way to improve margins through volume discounts or rebates from their suppliers?

You'll never know the exact answers to the questions above, but you can make educated guesses.

Now stitch together a compelling narrative about how each potential acquirer on your list could benefit from owning your business. The more convincing your story, the more value you will capture.

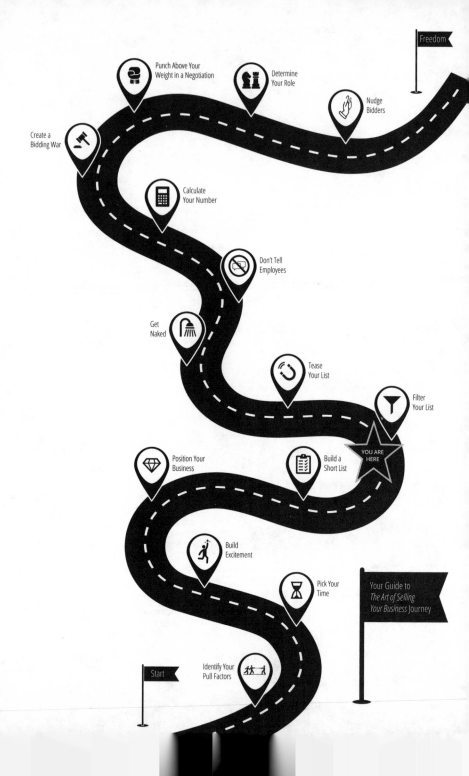

Freedom

Punch Above Your
Weight in a Negotiation

Determine
Your Role

Nudge
Bidders

Create a
Bidding War

Calculate
Your Number

Don't Tell
Employees

Get
Naked

Tease
Your List

Filter
Your List

YOU ARE
HERE

Position Your
Business

Build a
Short List

Your Guide to
*The Art of Selling
Your Business* Journey

Build
Excitement

Pick Your
Time

Start

Identify Your
Pull Factors

Chapter 8

THE 5-20 RULE

HOW TO ZERO IN ON YOUR
NATURAL ACQUIRER

Damien James grew up in Melbourne with two dreams for his life: playing for the Australian Football League (AFL) or building a successful business like his dad did. As his chances of making the AFL diminished with each passing year, he turned his attention to entrepreneurship.

James had read about the aging population in Australia and reasoned that health care was likely to be a lucrative field. He analyzed various options and discovered podiatry was a sector ripe for disruption.

Old people get sore feet, but nobody dies from a bunion, so the practice of podiatry is less regulated in Australia than some fields where medicine is a matter of life and death. At the time, most podiatrists in Melbourne worked from a retail location where the doctor owned and operated a private practice. The podiatrist would rent space, hire some staff, and charge patients per visit. At night, some enterprising doctors would also visit retirement communities to offer care. Reasoning that many elderly people nod off shortly after dinner, James saw an opportunity for a podiatrist to visit these patients during the day, when it was more convenient for them.

James, who had earned a bachelor's degree in podiatry in 1996, started Aged Foot Care. He approached senior care homes, suggesting a visit during the day. With a compelling offer and none of the traditional overhead of an office, he had discovered his million-dollar idea.

Aged Foot Care went through a variety of growing pains over the years, including an expensive rebranding to the name Dimple. By 2015, Dimple was generating roughly $200,000 of profit on $2.5 million in annual revenue in Australian dollars.[29]

Despite his success, James was frustrated. The company's growth had stalled, and his management team seemed perpetually incapable of hitting their targets. Quarter after quarter, he would set goals with his team, only to see them fall short. James decided it was time to bring in outside help, so he hired a recruiting firm to look for a chief operating officer. After interviewing a variety of candidates, James settled on Nick Beckett, who had just come off a successful

---

29 In 2015, the Australian dollar was worth approximately $0.73 USD.

run growing a tea company called T2, which had been acquired by Unilever in 2013.

To recruit Beckett, James knew he would need to give up some equity, so he commissioned a valuation for Dimple, which came in at $2.5 million. He offered Beckett a salary plus 5% of the company. James estimated he could get to $5 million in yearly revenue without Beckett's help, so he offered Beckett another 3% of the business (up to a maximum of 20%) for every $1 million Beckett grew Dimple's valuation past $5 million, capped at a maximum of $10 million, which would mean a 20% total share for Beckett.

The partnership got off to a fast start. Beckett started to employ the strategies he had used to grow T2 25-fold in 10 years. To his credit, James realized what he had in Beckett and quickly promoted him to chief executive officer. James stepped back from day-to-day operations to refocus on being a great founder, which proved to be a powerful catalyst for change when combined with Beckett's leadership as CEO.

Down to just one day a week, James shifted his responsibilities as founder to center around providing a strategic vision and reinforcing the company's core values. Beckett ran the day-to-day business, continuing to pursue James's core strategy of contracting with senior care facilities, and the company hit $11 million in revenue by 2017.

Around that time, Zenitas appeared on the scene. Zenitas had a similar strategy of bringing health care to patients in homes or care centers rather than having them languish in hospital beds. The company was keen to add podiatry to its stable of services, and acquiring Dimple would allow it to become a market leader almost overnight. Zenitas was expecting more than $65 million in revenue for

2017, so they were roughly six times larger than Dimple. By adding Dimple's $11 million in sales, they would crest $76 million for the year.

In July 2017, Zenitas announced they had acquired Dimple for $13.4 million. Under Beckett's day-to-day leadership, the company had grown in value over 500% in less than three years.[30]

James's story illustrates a few essentials I covered in *Built to Sell: Creating a Business That Can Thrive Without You*—like developing a business that can run once you're out of the picture, establishing a durable competitive advantage and finding a strategic acquirer with a compelling reason to buy your business. It also serves to demonstrate who the natural buyers are for a company, which can help you take the long list you developed in the previous chapter and winnow it down to something more manageable.

THE 5-20 RULE OF THUMB

So how long is your list of potential acquirers?

Remember, there is a sweet spot in any auction: the number that balances the probability of attracting multiple offers with the disruption and inevitable confidentiality breaches caused by a widescale auction. If you feel like you need to do some pruning, one of the best ways to shorten your list is to apply the 5-20 Rule: the most

---

30   John Warrillow, "How One Key Hire Helped Dimple Up Their Value by 500% in 2.5 Years," *Built to Sell Radio*, podcast, April 6, 2018, https://builttosell.com/radio/episode-134/

likely buyer for your company is often 5 to 20 times the size of your business today.[31]

Let's break down the 5-20 Rule into its two components, starting with the premise that your natural acquirer is likely to be at least five times the size of your company. Why does an acquirer have to be so much larger? Whatever happened to the idea of a "merger of equals"?

Acquiring a business can be a risky proposition, and buyers understand this. When they make a play for your company, they need to know that if it fails, it won't bring down their entire business. There is also the obvious fact that a company needs to be substantially larger than yours to have the cash (or the ability to borrow it) in order to buy you.

Imagine two potential acquirers of a $5-million business. Both buyers have an EBITDA margin of 10%, are in the same industry, and have identical reasons to purchase your business. The only difference is, Company A has $5 million in annual revenue and Company B has $25 million. Even though both have the same profit margin, Company B has five times more cash to finance an acquisition—and thus the buffer to ride out any hiccups that might arise as they integrate your business with theirs.

---

31 Thanks to Maryland-based M&A professional Todd Taskey for teaching me about the 5-20 Rule.

WHY NO MORE THAN 20 TIMES THE SIZE?

Now let's look at the second part of the 5-20 Rule, which is that your natural acquirer is not likely to be much more than 20 times your size.

This comes down to the simple fact that most companies with an appetite to acquire businesses can digest only a small number of acquisitions per year, and they would rather spend time on the ones that will actually make a difference.

Let's imagine you're running a mature company with $5 billion in annual sales and your board expects you to grow revenue by 10%. That's an increase of $500 million. You wipe your brow and get to work.

You could push your sales team's quotas up, but they'll start to rebel if you go too far. You might raise prices, but customers will start leaving if you're too aggressive. You could launch a new product, but that will take years to develop and test. So instead of relying entirely on organic growth, you figure you'll get at least part of your revenue increase through acquisitions.

You tell your corporate development leader that you want to bring on at least $100 million of the $500 million in growth you need through acquisitions. The corporate development team can deliver only one or two deals a year, so they look to buy larger companies that can make an impact.

You could have the world's best $5-million business, but it's still unlikely to gain the attention of a $5-billion giant, no matter how well you fit together strategically. Staffing, attorneys, certified public accountants (CPAs), and all the costs associated with research, due diligence, and closing on a sale are roughly the same for a business—whether the acquired company has $5 million or $50 million in annual revenue. For a $5-billion giant looking to acquire, it's only logical (and economical) to seek a single, larger acquisition.

The 5-20 Rule allows you to filter your long list and identify the companies most likely willing to make an acquisition offer. However, think of it as a "rule of thumb" rather than a law that is written in stone. There are examples of acquisitions that fall outside the 5-20 Rule, but they are somewhat unusual. You don't need to take a potential acquirer off your list just because they fall outside of the 5-20 Rule. Just know that an acquisition offer from them would be somewhat unusual.

TAKING ACTION

Take the long list of potential acquirers you developed in chapter 7 and winnow it down using the 5-20 Rule.

If you're not sure how much revenue a company generates, use $100,000 per employee as a very rough estimate. For example, if you know a company has around 100 employees, assume its revenue is roughly $10 million. While that guess may be way off, it will put you in the right zip code, which is all you need at this point.

Depending on how broad or targeted you intend to make your auction, you can also choose to include some companies outside of your 5-20 Rule, provided you realize their chances of making an offer are considerably lower.

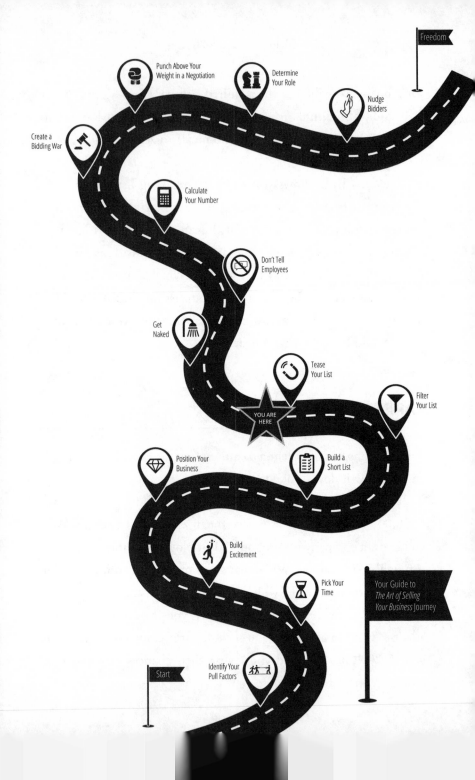

Freedom

Punch Above Your
Weight in a Negotiation

Determine
Your Role

Nudge
Bidders

Create a
Bidding War

Calculate
Your Number

Don't Tell
Employees

Get
Naked

Tease
Your List

Filter
Your List

YOU ARE
HERE

Position Your
Business

Build a
Short List

Build
Excitement

Pick Your
Time

Your Guide to
*The Art of Selling
Your Business* Journey

Start

Identify Your
Pull Factors

Chapter 9

THE TEASE

HOW TO ATTRACT ACQUIRERS
WITHOUT LOOKING DESPERATE

Among other things, Entrepreneurs' Organization organizes peer groups of business owners who meet once a month to share experiences with one another. As we took a break during one month's EO meeting, my forum mate, Sam, reached inside his pocket and pulled out a small square of paper. He unfolded it to reveal a dog-eared document with well-worn grooves in the folds. He started to read, making small notes as he scanned the paper.

I had seen Sam study this sheet before. Curious, I asked him what he was looking at.

"It's my VisualSonics teaser," Sam said, referring to the company in which he was a considerable shareholder.

Sam went on to explain that this one-page document described his business in sufficient detail to "tease" his short list of potential acquirers into learning more about his company. This type of document is called a "teaser" because the name of your company is not revealed, but enough information is shared to tempt a potential buyer to execute an NDA so they can learn more about your business.

Acquirers don't like signing NDAs for no reason, as it can open them up to litigation. So they're selective. Your teaser's job is to intrigue an acquirer on your short list to the point where they are willing to sign an NDA.

My friend Sam had no immediate plans to sell his company, but he was always tweaking his teaser—continuously fine-tuning how he would present his business to acquirers when he was ready.

In the end, Sam did sell VisualSonics for a cool $80 million, which began his journey to becoming Canada's largest venture capitalist in the medical technology sector, with $200 million of capital invested.

CRAFTING YOUR TEASER

If selling a business is a form of art, and if every great piece of art tells a story, think of your teaser as your introduction. It's a written summary of your business that positions it in the mind of an acquirer.

Typical sections include those listed below.

Summary

Start with a short description of your business, positioning your company in an industry that you know acquirers are keen on. Think of this as a 30-second commercial, but instead of selling your product, you're selling your company. Your summary should succinctly answer questions like the following:

- What product and/or service do you sell?
- How do you make money?
- When was your company founded?
- What industries do you sell to?
- What is your distribution model?

Remember that your summary should be sufficiently vague to ensure your company name is not obvious to the reader.

Financial highlights

Include a couple of financial highlights such as your revenue, growth rate, gross margin, and adjusted[32] EBITDA margin over the past few years. Also include a projection for revenue and EBITDA over the next two years.

---

32 "Adjustments" are the changes you make to your Profit & Loss statement in order to show how the company would perform in someone else's hands. For example, you would change the expense item for your salary and bonus with a market-rate salary for a manager who could do your job. See chapter 16 for more information on this process.

Investment highlights

What makes your company unique, and how can you defend that advantage? Focus on the strategic reasons your short-listed companies would want to buy your business. If you have a blue-chip list of clients, describe them; if you have a great location, mention that; if your product is world-beating, now is the time to thump your chest and describe why. This is a good place to include a description of any proprietary technology you've developed or intellectual property (IP) you've protected.

As you write, be careful to avoid bad clichés like "once-in-a-lifetime opportunity." Stick with the facts.

Team of employees

Make the case that your business is run by a competent team and that it's not just you. Include a summary of your team's composition, such as how many full- and part-time employees you have; the average employee tenure in years; and a list of management staff (sales, production, HR, etc.), noting those who will remain with the company after the acquisition. Do not include any employee names.

Reason for the transaction

Clearly state your goals for the transaction. This may be obvious to you, but there can be a lot of reasons owners sell all or part of their company. For example, are you looking to sell 100% of your business to retire? Or are you looking to sell a minority interest in your business to fund a growth idea or buy out a partner?

HOW TO EXPLAIN WHY YOU'RE SELLING

Since your teaser will include a reason for the proposed transaction, and it will come up again as you meet prospective buyers in person, we need to address how you should answer the obvious question that will be on every acquirer's mind: "Why are you selling?"

There is no right way to answer this question, but there are a lot of *wrong* ways to address it. Saying something like "I'm tired of this business," "I think we're at our peak," "I'm burnt out," or "I want to cash out" may be true, but you don't need to tell an acquirer that. Who in their right mind would want to buy a business that has reached its peak?

Remember, the art of selling your business is credibly telling a story about your company, and while your teaser may be compelling, there will still be a nagging question in the mind of the buyer: "If this business is so great, why do you want to sell it?"

You have to thread the needle between telling the truth and not sabotaging your sale. In addition, most acquirers will want to keep you involved in your business after a transaction, so you have to somehow explain why you're selling and at the same time assure the buyer that you are willing to help them monetize what they have acquired.

Private equity buyers will likely want you to hold a considerable amount of equity for years into the future. Strategic acquirers—especially if yours is a service business—may want you to stay on and run your company as a division of theirs for a few years. Individual investors will want to know that you'll be available to help them learn the ropes. In all cases, you have to communicate your level of willingness to help with a transition.

So if you want out, you have to find a way to say that without sounding like you're escaping a burning building. Here's a rough guide of what to say, based on your situation:

Your Situation	What You Can Say
You're tired, sick of managing employees, and burnt out. You have some new and exciting things you want to go do. You want to hand the keys to a buyer and run the other way.	"I'm really good at starting businesses, but scaling them has never been my strength. I'd like to find someone who can take what we've started and build it into something great."
You're ready to retire or your health is starting to suffer.	"While I've still got a lot of passion for my business and energy to support a transition, I'm at an age where I'm starting to think about retirement."
You want to cash out, but you're willing to hold some of your equity and remain involved as a shareholder after a transaction (i.e., a private equity deal).	"We're at a point where we'd like to find a partner with the financial and strategic resources to help us capitalize on the opportunities in front of us. For me, I'd like to diversify my personal balance sheet a bit, but I'd very much like to remain a significant shareholder going forward."
You've been approached with an unsolicited acquisition offer, and you're curious who else might be interested in buying your business.	"We're not looking to sell, but we've been approached by an acquirer. Before we go too far down the road with them, we wanted to look at where the strategic fit might be the strongest."
You want to attract an investor, but you'd be open to an outright acquisition.	"We're looking for a strategic partner who can help us get to the next level, and we're open to structuring a deal in whatever way makes the most sense."

TAKING ACTION

Prepare an anonymous teaser that describes your company as if it were a product you're trying to sell. Consider both the features of your business (its attributes) and the benefits an acquirer will enjoy by owning it.

Rehearse your answer to the question "Why do you want to sell?" so that you can deliver your response authentically and without hesitation. Your answer should be truthful and at the same time communicate that you're not racing for the exit.

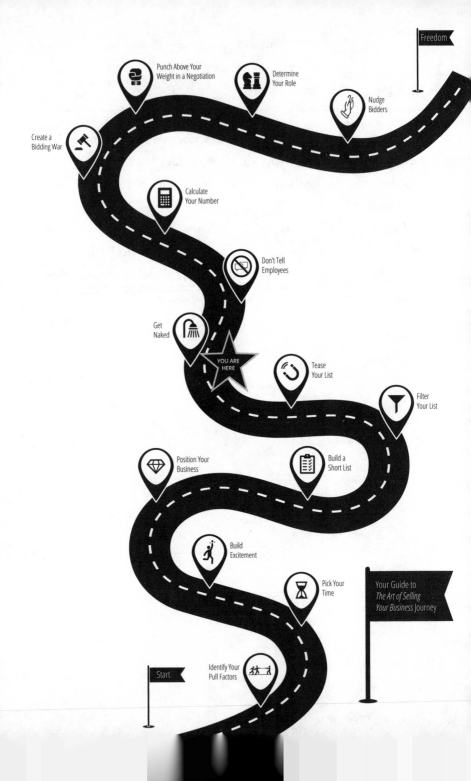

Freedom

Punch Above Your
Weight in a Negotiation

Determine
Your Role

Nudge
Bidders

Create a
Bidding War

Calculate
Your Number

Don't Tell
Employees

Get
Naked

YOU ARE
HERE

Tease
Your List

Filter
Your List

Position Your
Business

Build a
Short List

Build
Excitement

Pick Your
Time

Your Guide to
*The Art of Selling
Your Business* Journey

Start

Identify Your
Pull Factors

Chapter 10

GETTING (ALMOST) NAKED

HOW TO WRITE A CONFIDENTIAL INFORMATION MEMORANDUM

James Murphy started Lifes2Good in 1997 to import various creams and lotions into Ireland and the United Kingdom. It was a simple distribution business: find a product that sells well in another country, and negotiate the rights to sell it in the UK and Ireland.

In 2002, Murphy bought a distribution company with the rights to sell a hair-loss treatment called Viviscal. The company came with a list of 5,000 Viviscal customers. Murphy scanned the names on the list and noticed something odd: more than half of Viviscal's customers were women.

Murphy assumed a hair-loss treatment would appeal exclusively to men, but as he started to dig into the business, he discovered that women also deal with thinning hair. The reason for men's hair loss tended to be genetic, but Murphy learned that women usually lose their hair because of a hormonal imbalance or environmental factors like stress. While Viviscal didn't seem to make much difference for men, it was very successful at fighting hair loss among women.

As Murphy learned more about hair loss among women, he became increasingly interested in Viviscal. In 2007, he got a phone call from the owner of the Viviscal brand and formula, who asked whether Murphy would be interested in going beyond just owning the rights to distribute Viviscal in one region, and buying the business itself. Murphy's distribution company was generating less than €1 million[33] in Viviscal sales, and Murphy knew that if he owned the brand rather than just the rights to distribute it, he could build a much more valuable company.

Murphy acquired Viviscal and set out to build it into a significant player in the hair-loss category. Over the next 10 years, he commissioned 12 pharmaceutical-grade clinical trials to prove Viviscal's efficacy. Murphy won celebrity endorsements from the likes of Jennifer Aniston and Gwyneth Paltrow. He built a subscription service, eventually generating 30% of his revenue from recurring customers.

By 2017, Viviscal enjoyed 20% EBITDA margins on €50 million in sales, and Murphy decided it was the right time to sell. He began by hiring a US-based investment-banking firm that put together

---

33   In 2007, the euro was worth approximately $1.40 USD.

a confidential information memorandum (CIM). While the CIM included facts about Viviscal's sales and margins, it did not share details about the active ingredient in Viviscal.

The investment bankers approached a group of companies from the United States, Europe, the UK, and China that might have an interest in acquiring Viviscal. After Murphy received 12 bids ranging from €103 million to €115 million, he flew to New York, where he and his management team met with all 12 bidders in individual daylong meetings over two weeks.

Murphy started to winnow down the 12 original bidders to a short list. He dismissed the private equity firms and venture capitalists that were offering complex earnout schemes reliant on Murphy and his team to stay after the sale. Murphy knew a consumer packaged goods (CPG) company would have the most to gain in buying his business, because they could insert Viviscal into their massive distribution network.

He continued to play the remaining acquirers off one another. As the bidding got higher, companies started dropping out. Eventually, Murphy got the bidding up to €130 million. The list was down to just two CPG companies, one of which was Church & Dwight (C&D), the owner of brands like Arm & Hammer and Trojan. The two finalists were poring over the business, and at one point, Murphy estimated that more than 100 people from C&D were analyzing Viviscal.

The two finalists knew everything there was to know about Viviscal except one specific thing: the marine protein that made Viviscal so effective for the women who used it. Murphy, fearing the loss of his negotiating leverage if he revealed the formula to either company, kept his secret sauce confidential.

Finally, on January 24, 2017, C&D announced they had acquired

Viviscal for €150 million.[34] Only after the money cleared Murphy's bank account did C&D get the secret formula.

THE CONFIDENTIAL INFORMATION MEMORANDUM

In the acquisition process so far, you've positioned your company for a list of potential acquirers and sent them a teaser to tempt them into signing an NDA in return for more detailed information about your company.

Now you have to—as the great Patrick Lencioni said in his book of the same name—"get naked" and provide the potential buyer with a detailed package of information about your business. M&A professionals refer to this as a confidential information memorandum (CIM), a confidential information presentation (CIP), or simply "the book." The purpose of your CIM is to provide the acquirer with enough information to generate an initial offer, called a letter of intent (LOI), to acquire your business. (You will learn more about LOIs in chapter 14.)

Think of your CIM as a detailed brochure about your company. It should include facts about your business, communicated in a way that illustrates the magic behind what you have created.

While your CIM is an information packet, it's also a marketing document. Remember that great marketing always includes both features

---

34 John Warrillow, "How Jennifer Aniston and Reese Witherspoon Helped Viviscal Exit for 15 x EBITDA," *Built to Sell Radio*, podcast, June 15, 2018, https://builttosell.com/radio/episode-141/

and benefits. As legendary Harvard Business School marketing professor Theodore Levitt put it, customers (in your case, acquirers) want to "hire" a product to do a job. "People don't want to buy a quarter-inch drill," he explained. "They want a quarter-inch hole!"[35]

What "job" will your company allow an acquirer to get done? Your CIM should include sections on the following:

- Your business and its operations
  - o What makes your business model unique?
  - o What do you do better than your competitors?
  - o What have you figured out that an acquirer could leverage?

- Products and suppliers
  - o List your company's products and services, organized by percentage of annual revenue.
  - o List your products and services, organized by percentage of gross margin or cost of goods sold (or COGS).
  - o Rank your top three to five suppliers, noting how much you spend annually with each.

- Sales and marketing
  - o How does your company win a new customer?
  - o How much does it cost to acquire a new customer?

---

35 Clayton M. Christensen, Scott Cook, and Taddy Hall, "What Customers Want from Your Products," *Harvard Business Review*, January 16, 2006, https://hbswk.hbs.edu/item/what-customers-want-from-your-products

- o How predictable is your marketing engine?
- o How much market share have you captured?
- o How could an acquirer benefit from your sales and marketing approach?
- o If you have a recurring billing model, include statistics on churn rates and lifetime value of a customer.

- Barriers to entry
  - o What makes you unique and difficult for competitors to compete with?
  - o Have you legally protected any of your ideas—for example, through trademarks or patents?
  - o What would someone have to invest in terms of time and money to build what you've created?
  - o How would an acquirer benefit from the barriers to entry you have erected?

- Trends and opportunities in your industry
  - o What's exciting about your industry?
  - o What part of your sector is growing?
  - o Where is your industry going, and how well are you positioned to take advantage of these trends?
  - o How could an acquirer benefit from the latest developments in your sector?

- Financials
  - o Include adjusted Profit & Loss (P&L) statements for the past three years and projections for the next two.

- o Make sure you adjust your expenses (and income) to remove any one-time expenses a new buyer would not incur.
- o Replace your compensation expense (salary and bonus) with a market-rate salary for a general manager who could do what you do today.

- Your customers
  - o Describe your current customers. (Do *not* provide customer contact information or names of identifiable individuals. In fact, depending on how small your industry is, you may only feel comfortable providing a generic description of your customers.)
  - o What customers could you possibly reach if you had more resources?
  - o What markets could you enter if you had more resources?
  - o What products could you launch if you had more resources?
  - o What benefits would an acquirer enjoy by getting unfettered access to your customers?

- Your management team
  - o Describe how well your company would run without you.
  - o Show a visual organization chart that includes low and high compensation ranges for each employment area or division.
  - o Include a bio of each person in a leadership position

in the company (including current compensation and incentives, if any).

o Detail each leader's scope of responsibility.

o How would an acquirer benefit from having your managers join their team?

THE RISK OF GETTING NAKED

Developing and sharing your CIM is a tricky stage in the process of selling your business, because you have to reveal some of the most intimate details about your company for an audience that may not have the best intentions. While you need to reveal enough for a well-meaning acquirer to make an offer, some unscrupulous executives will sign an NDA just to get proprietary information about your business, and there's not much you can do about it.

Consider the story of Dinesh Dhamija, who started UK-based ebookers.com, a website European travelers use to book trips. Dhamija launched the site from his brick-and-mortar travel agency in 1999. By 2005, ebookers was doing more than $1 *billion* in annual sales.[36]

The online travel industry works on commissions negotiated with hotels and airlines. The more volume you have, the more negotiating leverage you get to push for a fatter cut. Commission rates are a tightly guarded secret in the industry because if they were made

---

36   John Warrillow, "A $471 Million Exit From the Online Travel Industry," *Built to Sell Radio*, podcast, August 9, 2019, https://builttosell.com/radio/episode-193/

public, it would give competitors leverage in their own discussions with the travel operators.

When Dhamija decided to sell ebookers, he prepared a CIM that included the commission rates he had negotiated. Given ebookers' success, he quickly got six of the largest online travel sites in the world to sign NDAs in return for his CIM.

Two of the six companies made him an offer to buy the business. When I interviewed Dhamija, I asked about the other four companies. He responded that he discovered later "they weren't interested in making an offer. They just wanted to know the commission rates we had negotiated."

In Dhamija's case, revealing private information to his competitors was a calculated risk he was willing to take to sell his business—which he did, to Cendant (the owner of Avis and Orbitz, among many other brands), for a cool $471 million.

It worked out for Dhamija, but had he not been successful in attracting an offer, he would have been left wounded by the process of putting his business up for sale. Depending on your circumstances, there may be something so proprietary—as in the case of James Murphy and Viviscal—that you have to leave it out of the CIM.

Even when a potential acquirer signs an NDA, it is very difficult to prove that they improved their business using proprietary information they learned through reading your CIM. Sharing such information is a calculated risk you take, which is why you don't want to put your business on the market unless you're fully committed to seeing it through—and why you sign a mutual NDA only with reputable companies you believe have a genuine interest in making an offer.

TAKING ACTION

Pull together the information you'll need to write your CIM. Ponder the features of your business as well as the benefits an acquirer will enjoy by owning it.

Resign yourself to getting (mostly) naked. You'll need to provide details about your operations, finances, sales and marketing, etc.

Consider whether there is anything so proprietary that you will choose to keep it private—even at the risk of losing out on a deal.

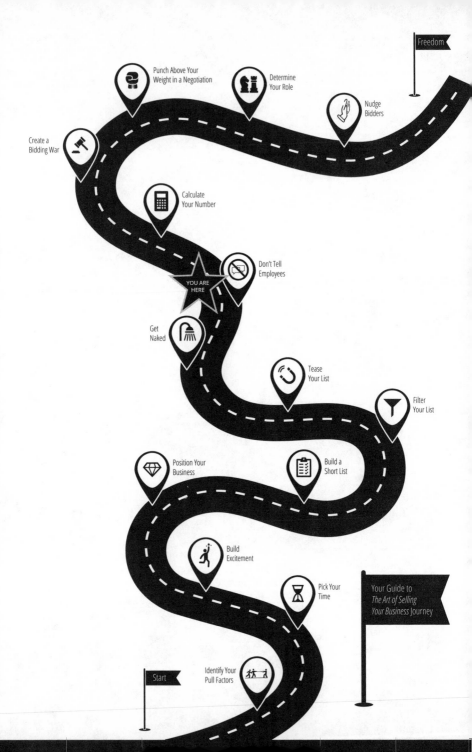

Freedom

Punch Above Your Weight in a Negotiation

Determine Your Role

Nudge Bidders

Create a Bidding War

Calculate Your Number

Don't Tell Employees

YOU ARE HERE

Get Naked

Tease Your List

Filter Your List

Position Your Business

Build a Short List

Build Excitement

Pick Your Time

Your Guide to *The Art of Selling Your Business* Journey

Start

Identify Your Pull Factors

Chapter 11

KEEPING YOUR SECRET

How (and When) to Tell
Your Employees

Built to Sell had just been published, and I'd been hired by a bank to speak to some of their business clients. A question-and-answer period was built into my talk, and I'd anticipated the grilling I would get. I imagined the audience asking about how companies are valued or how to create recurring revenue, so I was surprised by the first question: "How should I tell my employees that I'm planning to sell the company?"

Since that first speech, I've given lots of talks to business owners, and the question of how and when to tell employees is almost always one of the first things I get asked about.

Right vs. Best

Unfortunately, how and when to tell employees that you're thinking of selling is one of life's imperfect moments—and the *right* answer may not always be the *best* answer. If you're like most founders, you rely deeply on your people and have a tremendous sense of loyalty to the employees who have helped you get where you are.

If you foster a transparent culture and you decide to sell, you'll start feeling like a cheating spouse, skulking around the office with a giant secret nobody knows about. The guilt may even become paralyzing.

The morally "right" answer is to tell your team—but that is one of the single biggest mistakes you can make in selling your company. This book is about your endgame, and randomly telling your employees you're considering selling is almost always a catastrophic mistake. Here's why.

Some deals fall apart.

Some businesses that are listed for sale never sell. Some deals even get as far as a letter of intent and then dissolve during due diligence, well before a definitive purchase agreement is ever negotiated. The last thing you want to do is tell your employees, only to have them panic for no reason—which leads me to the second reason not to divulge your intentions too soon.

Employees get rattled when they know you're selling.

Your employees will have heard stories of people who got laid off when their employer sold the company. Yet the reality is, most acquirers will need your employees to remain so they can capture the value they're buying when they purchase your business.

As a matter of fact, in most cases, your employees' jobs are probably never more secure than immediately following an acquisition. Even so, your team will most likely start polishing their resumes as soon as you tell them you're selling. Why give them any reason to worry unnecessarily?

Panicky employees often leak the news to industry people.

Upon hearing the news that you're selling, where do you think your employees will look for a new job? Keen to leverage their industry experience, some may approach your competitors for a job, which will tip off your industry peers. This could compromise your position in the market in the eyes of customers and sabotage your sale.

If your results slide, expect your price to go along with it.

An acquirer's due diligence can last many months, and if your employees are distracted, your business will likely suffer. If your results turn south during diligence, prepare for a buyer to ask for a discount on their purchase price.

Deals morph as they progress.

What starts as an acquisition discussion may change into a strategic partnership. If your employees are fixated on a sale, that can compromise your flexibility to negotiate a great partnership.

You'll need everyone on board to hit your earnout.

An acquirer may structure their acquisition offer with part of your proceeds tied to an earnout, which could last anywhere from one to seven years. You'll need your team to help you achieve your earnout. While you may be selling your ownership stake, nothing much changes for your employees when you continue to run your business as a division of the acquiring company.

You may decide not to sell.

You could go through the entire process of marketing your business for sale and then simply change your mind. In such a situation, your decision not to sell may be a big distraction for your employees. Discussing a sale that never comes to fruition is likely to cause confusion—and put your loyalty and commitment to your business in question.

YOUR END OF THE BARGAIN

This book is about the art of negotiating your sale for the highest possible price. I'll leave it to others to comment on the morally right time to inform your employees of your decision to sell, but I will ask you to consider the following set of questions before you get swallowed up by guilt:

- Do you pay a market-rate wage?
- Do you offer employees a safe working environment?
- Do you promote people when they do well and provide coaching to those who are struggling?

- Do you provide decent benefits?

- Did you personally risk much or all of your life savings to create your business?

- Were there occasions when you sacrificed time with friends and family because your company needed you?

If your answer to all of those questions is "yes," then you've delivered on your end of the employment bargain, and you don't *owe* your employees advance notice of a potential sale. No, not all of your employees will see it that way, and some will feel betrayed when they find out you have sold. In my view, that is their problem—not yours.

TWO EMPLOYEE CATEGORIES

Let's cast aside the moral debate about what's right and focus on what is strategically sound. If you can stomach it, my recommendation is to divide your employees into two categories and treat each one according to what is best for the business.

The first category contains employees who are senior leaders whom you must tell in order to get the deal done. Your acquirer will want to talk to your management team at some point, and these are the people who need to know what's going on. Have them agree to keep the possible sale confidential, and give them some financial incentive for helping you close the deal.

Most owners assume they have to give away stock in order for managers to benefit from a sale, but giving your employees stock or options at this late stage may just muddy the process and over-complicate things. Consider a simple "stay" or "success" bonus that you'll pay on a successful transaction. I would recommend you pay that bonus in two parts: one immediately following a successful sale, and the second part a year after—provided these people are still employed with your company.[37] That way, your managers are less likely to walk out the door immediately after the sale.

The second category is made up of your rank-and-file employees who should be told once your bank has received the acquirer's wire transfer. Yes, the news at this late stage will ruffle some feathers. Yes, you may damage some relationships. But in the end, it's simply the price of getting a deal done.

For an example of owners who—as hard as it was—did this well, let's look at Lois and Ross Melbourne, who started Aquire Solutions, a software business that helped large companies manage their employees.

The Melbournes had self-funded their business over 18 years, eventually growing it to 85 people, when they received an offer from a private equity firm rolling up software companies in the human resources field. The offer represented enough money for the couple to permanently retire in their forties. There was only one problem: how to tell their staff—whom they thought of as family members—that they were selling out.

The Melbournes decided to tell their employees on a "need to know" basis. Senior managers who participated in the negotiation

---

37   I'm not a lawyer, so make sure you get a lawyer familiar with the laws in your area to prepare any agreements.

were told and sworn to secrecy. The rest of the staff were told after the deal had closed.

As Lois Melbourne told me when I interviewed her for *Built to Sell Radio*, she felt conflicted throughout the sale process. She was used to being transparent with her staff, and yet everywhere she went, she was carrying this secret around with her.[38] The stress led Melbourne to break down in tears when she finally told her staff they had sold the business.

Years later, the Melbournes now see their former staff members around town, and there are no hard feelings. The Melbournes have even been invited to join a private Facebook group of former employees. As time has passed, employees have gotten over the initial shock and realized that in keeping the sale quiet, the Melbournes were doing what they had to do for the success of the sale—and for the good of the business.

Telling your staff you are thinking of selling may feel like the right thing to do, but in the end, keeping them in the dark may be the best thing for you *and your employees.*

---

38 John Warrillow, "When to Tell Employees You're Thinking of Selling," *Built to Sell Radio*, podcast, April 26, 2017, https://builttosell.com/radio/episode-89/

THE ONE (SORT OF) EXCEPTION TO THE RULE

There is one exception to the rule about not telling your employees too soon: if you have provided your employees a financial incentive for helping you sell, and you have been transparent all along about your desire to sell.

Glenn Grant built G2 Technology Group and told his 30 employees from the beginning (as far back as their first interview) that he would sell G2 one day. He offered each employee stock appreciation rights, which gave employees a stake in the value of G2 right from when they started.

Since all employees were motivated and incentivized by a sale, Grant chose to be transparent with employees when he received three offers to acquire G2—one of which he accepted, agreeing to sell G2 to Great Hill Partners in 2018.[39]

In telling his employees, who had a financial stake in the sale, Grant rolled the dice and won. But telling his team could have backfired—and it's not an approach I would typically recommend.

TAKING ACTION

Write a list of all of your employees, and categorize them into one of two categories: a small group of senior management who need to know now about your possible plans to sell the business, and a larger group of those who will find out after the transaction is complete.

---

39   John Warrillow, "Multiple of Earnings vs. Revenue," *Built to Sell Radio*, podcast, September 6, 2019, https://builttosell.com/radio/episode-197/

Next, design an incentive for the small group of managers who need to know, and prepare a document describing that success bonus and how it is contingent on keeping the sale confidential.

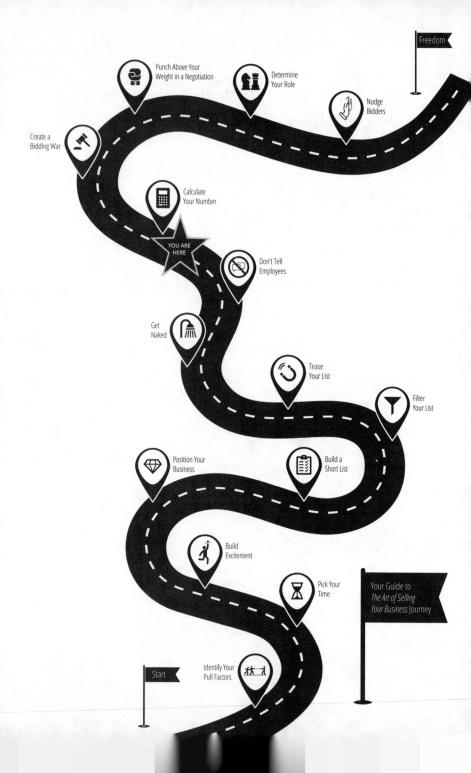

Freedom

Punch Above Your Weight in a Negotiation

Determine Your Role

Nudge Bidders

Create a Bidding War

Calculate Your Number

YOU ARE HERE

Don't Tell Employees

Get Naked

Tease Your List

Filter Your List

Position Your Business

Build a Short List

Build Excitement

Pick Your Time

Your Guide to
The Art of Selling Your Business Journey

Start

Identify Your Pull Factors

Chapter 12

WHAT'S YOUR
NUMBER?

HOW TO CALCULATE
YOUR BOTTOM LINE

Kris Jones founded Pepperjam, a digital marketing agency that he
grew into a successful business with a differentiated technology
platform, which his team had built for managing affiliate advertising campaigns. Given its unique technology, Pepperjam piqued the
curiosity of Michael Rubin, founder and CEO of GSI, a company
that created online stores for some of the world's best-known brands
before it was acquired by eBay.

As Jones told me during our *Built to Sell Radio* interview,[40] Rubin cultivated a relationship with Jones over some months. Then he called Jones into his Philadelphia headquarters. Jones was expecting to walk into a one-on-one with Rubin, so he was surprised to find Rubin had gathered his chief marketing officer, chief financial officer, and legal counsel in the boardroom.

Without even so much as an exchange of pleasantries, Rubin asked the three-word question: "What's your price?"

Jones was surprised. He had expected a casual conversation between two technology entrepreneurs but felt as if he had just walked into the lion's den. It was four on one, and Jones was on the spot.

Jones hesitated and then blurted out his number.

Rubin's response: "I think we can get a deal done."

Jones went on to close the sale with Rubin for almost exactly the price he had uttered in that boardroom. Ultimately Jones considers his exit a success, but there will always be a part of him that wonders whether he could have gotten just a little more for his company had he forced Rubin to make the first offer.

FIGURING OUT YOUR NUMBER

What's your number?

Oh, don't be coy. You know the one.

I'm talking about the amount of money you would need to be offered to sell your business today.

40　John Warrillow, "The Ambush," *Built to Sell Radio*, podcast, May 11, 2016, https://builttosell.com/radio/episode-43/

While you should avoid revealing it to a buyer, my advice is to write your number down. As you progress through the stages of selling your business, your number will be tested and you may be tempted to change it. That can lead to disappointment later, when you reflect on your sale and wonder whether you got a reasonable price.

To calculate your number, you have to answer two questions:

1. What's your business worth?
2. What's your business worth *to you*?

Let's start with the first question.

WHAT'S YOUR BUSINESS WORTH?

Entire textbooks have been written on business valuation, and my intention is not to bore you with all the details. Let's just tackle the three most common ways you can estimate the value of your business. You can calculate the value of your assets, use a technique called discounted cash flow (DCF), or look at companies similar to yours and estimate what they're selling for.

Let's take a look at all three.

Assets

The most basic way to value your business is to figure out what your hard assets are worth and subtract any debt you have on your business.

Imagine a landscaping company with trucks and gardening equipment. These hard assets have value, which can be calculated by estimating the resale value of the equipment minus any debt.

This valuation method often renders the lowest value for your company because it assumes your company does not have any goodwill. In accountant speak, goodwill has nothing to do with how much people like your company; goodwill is defined as the difference between your company's market value (what someone is willing to pay for it) and the fair market value of your net assets (assets minus liabilities).

Typically, companies have at least some goodwill, so in most cases you'll get a higher valuation by using one of the other two methods described below.

Discounted cash flow

In this method, the acquirer is estimating what your future stream of cash flow is worth to them today. They start by trying to figure out how much profit you expect to make in the next few years. The more stable and predictable your cash flows, the more years of future cash they will consider.

Once the buyer has an estimate of how much profit you're likely to make in the foreseeable future, and what your business will be worth when they project selling it, the buyer will apply a "discount rate" that accounts for the time value of money. The discount rate is determined by the acquirer's cost of capital and how risky they perceive your business to be.

Rather than getting hung up on the math behind the DCF valuation technique, it's better to understand the drivers you can control when an acquirer uses this method. These are determined by your answers to the following questions:

1. How consistent have your profits been, and for how long?

2. How much profit do you expect to make in the future?

3. How reliable are those estimates?

You focus on those attributes, and let the propeller heads do the math.

Comparables

Another common valuation technique is to look at the value of similar companies that have sold recently or whose value is more or less public knowledge because of industry standards. For example, accounting firms typically trade at one times gross recurring fees. Home and office security companies trade at about two times monitoring revenue; most security company owners know the comparables technique because they often get approached by private equity firms rolling up small security firms. You can usually find out what companies in your industry are selling for by asking around at your annual industry conference.

The problem with using the comparables methodology is that it often leads owners to make an apples-to-bananas comparison. You may compare yourself with a similar company in your industry that just sold, but without an intimate understanding of their business, you may be drawing a comparison that isn't there. Private companies are just that—private. That means you can estimate things like their profit, gross margin, and growth rate, but unless you have insider knowledge, you will just be guessing.

So to avoid guessing, owners often look for public comparables information, which leads to comparing themselves to a large publicly traded company in the same industry—and that is a recipe for regret. For example, because medical technology companies generally trade for 20 times last year's earnings on the New York Stock Exchange (NYSE), a small medical device manufacturer might think they too are worth 20 times last year's profit. However, I can tell you, after analyzing tens of thousands of businesses that use The Value Builder System, a small medical device manufacturer is likely to trade at a fraction of 20 times. Small companies are deeply discounted when compared with their large, publicly traded counterparts, so measuring your company's value against a Fortune 500 giant will often lead to disappointment.

WHAT'S YOUR BUSINESS WORTH *TO YOU*?

The worst part about selling your business is that you don't get to decide *which* methodology the acquirer chooses. An acquirer will do the math behind closed doors on what your business is worth *to them*. They may decide your business is strategic, in which case you should back up the Brinks truck because you're about to get handsomely rewarded for your company. But in most cases, an acquirer will use one of the three techniques described here to come up with an offer to buy your company.

Perhaps a tougher question to answer is what's your business worth to you? One of the most common mistakes owners make in valuing their business is estimating how much money they need to retire and then using that figure to determine their selling price. The two numbers have nothing to do with one another. Just because you calculate you need $1 million to retire doesn't mean your business is worth that to an acquirer. By starting with your retirement nut, you're answering a different question—about the value of your business in no one's eyes but yours.

What your business is worth to you may have little bearing on its market value, but it can be the biggest determinant as to whether or not you sell. There are practical and philosophical ways to answer this question.

Practically, you probably generate an income and enjoy some benefits from owning your business, and you can calculate the cost of replacing that stream of cash. This kind of math can help determine what your business is worth *to you*, but will have no bearing on what it is worth to someone else. You need both numbers—and if you stick with me for a moment, you'll see why.

Philosophically, what your business is worth *to you* is a much trickier question. There are many intangible benefits to owning a business; these are hard to quantify. For example, what's it worth to be recognized as an important member in your community when you walk down Main Street on a Saturday morning? What's it worth to see a job well done, knowing you made it possible? How do you value the feeling of pride you get from employing someone who might have trouble finding a job elsewhere?

Similarly, owning a business involves a number of intangible costs that may drag down its value in your mind. For example, what does it cost you emotionally to worry about your business every day? What's the psychological toll of having to let someone go? What's the cost of the stress you endure knowing most of your net worth is tied up in your business? What's the price of having to check your mobile phone while you're on vacation?

Weigh these intangible benefits and costs, and do your best to calculate what your business is worth *to you*.

KNOWING WHEN TO SELL—HOW TO ANSWER *THE* QUESTION

The final step in the process is comparing the two numbers: what your company is worth to the outside world and what it's worth to you. When the value of your business to an outsider exceeds what it's worth to you personally at this point in your life, then it may be time to sell. Likewise, if your company is worth more to you than it would be worth to a buyer, putting it on the market now will be an exercise in frustration.

At some point in the negotiations to sell your business, most sophisticated buyers will try to extract your number from you. As Kris Jones discovered, smart buyers will often wait until you are alone, unprotected by your intermediary or legal counsel, who know better than to answer.

The query sounds so innocent: "So what do you want for your business?" Answering it directly, however, is almost always a mistake. If you blurt out your number, you will forever put a hard ceiling on what your company is worth in the eyes of the potential buyer. An acquirer will never pay a penny more than your number and will make it their mission to get your company for less.

Similarly, if your number is too high, you could turn off a potential buyer, who may conclude that you are unreasonable before you have the chance to weave your narrative about why your business is worth such a premium. You'll have lost the game before you even start.

When you get the question, simply demur by making it clear you're a fair person and would seriously consider any reasonable offer from an acquirer.

TAKING ACTION

Value your business using all three approaches to get a rough sense of what your company could be worth to a buyer. Then do the math and the soul searching to figure out what your company is worth *to you*. If it is worth more to a buyer than it is to you, now may be a good time to sell.

Keep your number to yourself. Just because you have one doesn't mean you need to share it. To avoid putting a ceiling on your value—or looking greedy before the dance with an acquirer has even begun—let the potential buyer make the first move.

Punching above Your Weight in a Negotiation

Selling your business can feel like a David-versus-Goliath battle. You may find yourself negotiating with a mercenary acquirer who makes a living from buying companies for less than they are worth. This section is packed with essential tips, countermeasures, and killer hacks for outmaneuvering and outflanking a professional buyer.

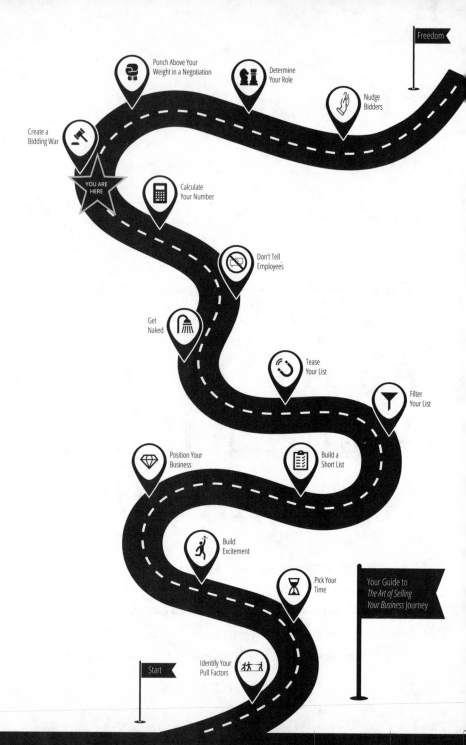

Freedom

Punch Above Your Weight in a Negotiation

Determine Your Role

Nudge Bidders

Create a Bidding War

YOU ARE HERE

Calculate Your Number

Don't Tell Employees

Get Naked

Tease Your List

Filter Your List

Position Your Business

Build a Short List

Build Excitement

Pick Your Time

Your Guide to *The Art of Selling Your Business* Journey

Start

Identify Your Pull Factors

also download *The Art of Selling Your Business*
learning to your business. Just pop your email

Chapter 13

BIDDING WAR

HOW TO GET MULTIPLE OFFERS

Arik Levy had a problem.

As a vice president at PNI Corporation, Levy needed a pressed shirt every morning, yet he was perpetually running out of clean garb.

The problem traced back to his dry cleaner's hours. By the time Levy left work most evenings, the cleaner had already closed. Sometimes Levy went days without clean laundry.

The inconvenience caused Levy to imagine a solution. He conceived of a locker system where a busy office worker could drop off dirty clothes for a dry cleaner to pick up. Once clean, the garments could be returned to the locker, which would then dispatch a text message letting the customer know the clean clothes were ready for pickup.

In 2005, Levy turned his dream into a reality by launching Laundry Locker, an early pioneer in the burgeoning business of supplying lockers for people who order stuff they need delivered.

Almost a decade later, Levy leveraged his experience in lockers for a new offering that targeted people who live in high-rise buildings. Levy reasoned that apartment dwellers were increasingly shopping online, but many buildings did not have a secure way to accept shipments from online retailers. Doormen were becoming glorified shipping and receiving clerks. In many buildings, packages were languishing for days, leaving both apartment owners and tenants frustrated. Levy envisioned a locker system that could be installed in a multi-tenant building, thus allowing residents to shop online and pick up their shipments from their lockers when they liked.

Levy named the new company Luxer One. He considered raising venture capital to fund its growth, but decided against it based on the challenges he had experienced when raising money in the past. In previous ventures, Levy had approached venture capital firms, only to have his meetings relegated to a junior associate who listened politely but wasn't empowered to invest. Levy found himself going around in circles and felt frustrated by the entire process of pitching investors.

This time, instead of raising money, Levy decided to get his customers to help him finance some of his growth. He began to aggressively build a portfolio of apartments, charging them 50% of the cost of the locker system upon signing an agreement, with the balance due on delivery. (Levy also charged an ongoing service fee to maintain the system.)

Using this innovative financing model, Levy grew Luxer One from $1 million in sales in 2014 to an incredible $37 million in 2018, without the dilution of a venture round.

That's when Levy was approached by a nationwide retailer who wanted to install Luxer One lockers in all of their stores. There was only one catch: they were not prepared to pay for the lockers up front and would only place their order if Levy agreed to accept payment 30 days after installation. Levy needed money to finance such a big order, but based on his experience raising money in the past, he was hesitant to pitch institutional investors.

It was around this time that Levy received an email from a customer named Trip Wolfe, who lived in a building where Luxer One lockers had recently been installed. Wolfe was impressed with the Luxer One model and, as an M&A professional with PricewaterhouseCoopers, offered to help Levy raise money for Luxer One if he ever needed the help.

Keen to fill the massive order from the nationwide retailer insisting on payment terms, Levy hired Wolfe to drum up interest in investing in Luxer One. Wolfe got to work and applied his expertise to the Luxer One opportunity. He helped Levy prepare his bookkeeping and forecast his growth. Together they developed a narrative of what Luxer One could become with the right partner. With a compelling teaser and CIM prepared, Wolfe took Luxer One to market.

Wolfe got interest from investors, but he also managed to attract five acquisition offers from strategic buyers who wanted to purchase Luxer One outright.

Levy ended up selling Luxer One to Assa Abloy AB, a Swedish

conglomerate with more than $9 billion in annual revenue.[41] Levy had heard of Assa Abloy but never considered them a potential acquirer. It was Wolfe who had suggested Levy add them to his short list.

ASK "WHO," NOT "HOW"

As the story of Arik Levy illustrates, the process of selling your company is not a do-it-yourself project. Levy struggled for months to raise capital, but when he brought in Wolfe to run a structured M&A process, he ended up with five appealing acquisition offers.

Drumming up offers for your company—as Dan Sullivan, the founder of The Strategic Coach, likes to say—is a "who," rather than a "how" question. Instead of investing time trying to figure out *how* you will reach your short list of potential acquirers, figure out *who* would be the very best person to do this on your behalf. In other words, at this point in the process it's time to hire an intermediary such as a business broker or a mergers and acquisitions professional.

I've chosen to wait until this point to introduce the role of an intermediary because I think it's important that you understand what they do. As with hiring any professional, you're in the best position to manage an intermediary if you know what they should be doing. That is why it's important that you first learn the entire process of packaging a business properly for sale. It doesn't mean

---

41   John Warrillow, "How to Avoid Getting Diluted," *Built to Sell Radio*, podcast, October 18, 2019, https://builttosell.com/radio/episode-203/

you have to do all the work, but you should know what the work is—and what it looks like when it is done well.

There are some amazing intermediaries out there (like Wolfe) and some lousy ones, so invest the time to find a good one who appreciates both the science and the art of selling a business. The first thing you'll need to kick off your search for an intermediary is to know the title of the person you're looking for.

BUSINESS BROKER VS. M&A PROFESSIONAL

What follows is a general outline of the different types of intermediaries. I've presented these as hard lines, but in reality, the distinctions between these individuals are blurry.

Business broker: Sells companies worth up to $10 million

A business broker is someone who sells smaller companies worth up to $10 million. Regular brokers list your business for sale on a few "business for sale" marketplaces and take a commission when your company sells. Brokers often target individual buyers to purchase the businesses they list.

"Quality Main Street business brokers" is a generic industry term that describes those brokers who focus on the upper end of the market by selling companies worth between $1 million and $10 million. Like most brokers, they take a commission when your business sells and may charge a fee to get your company ready to market. Quality Main Street business brokers target individuals, small PEGs, and strategic buyers to purchase the businesses they take to market.

M&A professional: Sells companies worth $10 million–$100 million

An M&A professional usually handles larger businesses they estimate are worth at least $10 million (although some have a minimum as low as $5 million). They charge a "success fee," which is industry lingo for a commission. This commission rate is usually smaller on a percentage basis than a broker's, but the overall dollar value of the commission is usually greater because M&A professionals sell more valuable companies. M&A professionals usually also charge a nonrefundable fee to get your business ready to go to market; this can often be deducted from their success fee.

M&A professionals usually have a list of PEGs they know are looking to invest in businesses, and they'll often market your company to strategic acquirers as well.

Investment banker: Sells companies worth $100 million-plus

If you think your business is worth more than $100 million, you'll be looking for an investment banker carrying a card from a bank whose name you probably recognize. They'll be searching for a large PEG or a strategic acquirer to buy your company.

Regardless of which intermediary you choose, find one for whom you will be neither their smallest nor their largest deal.

Next, look for someone who has sold a company similar to yours, but don't be limited to industry gurus. You're looking for someone who appreciates what makes your company great—and someone with whom you have a personal connection. You'll spend a lot of time together over the next few months, so make sure you have good rapport.

As with hiring any professional, call a few of the intermediary's references to get the scoop from other owners who used their services.

SELL SIDE VS. BUY SIDE

As if finding an intermediary isn't hard enough, you also have to ensure they are truly working for you. In M&A parlance, brokers can be working on either the "buy side" or the "sell side" of a transaction.

A sell-side intermediary is an individual who has been hired by a seller to find an acquirer for their company.

A buy-side broker has been hired by a company (or an individual) to find them a business to buy. Occasionally, some buy-side brokers are less than forthcoming about whom they are working for. Upon approaching you, they may even sound like they are offering to represent you in some way, but don't be fooled. They are working for the buyer.

To ensure a prospective intermediary would be working for you exclusively, simply ask if they are working on any buy-side mandates right now.

This problem of divided loyalties can also arise innocently when you choose to hire an intermediary with a strong focus on a specific industry where only a handful of acquirers exist. Chances are, if you hire an industry guru to represent you, the majority of their livelihood comes from selling businesses to a small group of companies. Since they need to maintain positive and constructive relationships with each buyer in the industry, they are less likely to push hard for an extraordinary deal for you. They want to avoid burning a bridge with any acquirers. In other words, being viewed as reasonable by the main acquirers in your industry may be more important to them than squeezing an acquirer for every last penny or deal point.

On the other hand, an intermediary with an industry specialty will typically be able to give you a good sense of what the going rate is for a business like yours, and will have the natural acquirers on speed dial—which means you're likely to get a deal done, provided you're not looking to attract an offer that is far outside any industry norms that the intermediary tells you are reasonable. For example, if an expert M&A professional specializing in your industry tells you the realistic range of value for your company is between five and six times adjusted EBITDA, don't hire them if you won't budge for a penny less than 10 times adjusted EBITDA.

THE TOOLS FOR REACHING OUT ARE CHANGING

There was a time when a travel agent was the only one who could recommend a good hotel. Now, however, online marketplaces have shrunk the travel agency industry to the point where only the superb agents with a specific niche can survive.

Similarly, real estate agents used to be the only ones who could efficiently find you a house, whereas these days, most buyers will discover their dream home online and tell their agent to book a showing. Not surprisingly, real estate agency commissions are trending down.

Even singles bars have all but disappeared as online dating websites have eliminated the need. All agents and middlemen—such as real estate and travel agents—have seen their roles diminish over time as online marketplaces have taken away information as a currency.

The business of selling companies is also evolving, with the proliferation of a variety of new online marketplaces to help buyers and sellers find each other. This doesn't mean intermediaries are becoming extinct, but it does mean the process of finding you a buyer is becoming somewhat more commoditized. Today, the real value added by an intermediary is found in the artful way they dance with potential acquirers.

GOING IT ALONE

Right about now, you may be asking why you need an intermediary. Many owners manage the process of selling their business on their own or with the help of an experienced lawyer, so why add another mouth to the trough?

I understand your thinking, but I still believe you need a good intermediary, for these six reasons:

1. **Create competition.** A good intermediary will create competition for your business and ensure that you're getting a fair price and terms. Over at The Value Builder System, we've conducted research[42] with former owners to

---

42   This research inspired a tool called PREScore™ that allows you to assess how ready you are to exit your business. You can get your PREScore at www.PreScore.com.

find out why they often regret their decision to sell, and one of the most common reasons is a sense they didn't get a fair price for their business. The best way to know if you got a reasonable price is to get more than one offer. If there is only one interested bidder for your business, you could make it appear as though you have multiple bidders—but a savvy acquirer will likely see through your facade, realize they are the only legitimate bidder at the table, and drop their price and harden their terms accordingly. To get the best possible price for your business, you need an experienced intermediary who will construct the *illusion* of competition.

2. **Keep acquirers interested.** Just as sellers want multiple bidders, acquirers want proprietary deals where they are the only buyer at the table. Some acquirers are so insistent on getting an exclusive deal that they will balk if they believe they are being asked to participate in a wide-scale auction with dozens of potential acquirers. Unless you have a truly incredible company (assume you don't, because as a founder, it is very hard for you to be objective on this), some acquirers may decline to participate in a broad auction. An intermediary who appreciates the art of selling will find the middle ground by alluding to competitive bidders while also making the potential acquirer feel as if they have been chosen from a short list. It's a fine line best toed by a professional.

3. **Provide a buffer.** Selling your business is personal (as I mentioned way back in chapter 2). In the beginning, potential acquirers will be on their best behavior and likely treat you as an industry luminary. You'll be bathed in com-

pliments and have the impression the acquirer thinks you walk on water. As your deal progresses, this warm embrace will be replaced by the cold, hard edges of professional negotiators. Every aspect of your business will be scrutinized and questioned by an acquirer, which will put you on the defense. Even the most zen-like sellers will get annoyed and take offense. That's when an intermediary can act as a buffer, deflecting or reframing some of the acquirer's most personal criticism so that it will be less likely to set you off in a huff.

4. **Be the good cop.** Not only can a good intermediary soften criticism of your business and be the glue that holds a deal together, they can also provide the hard edge to a negotiation when necessary. They can be your "bad cop" pushing back on deal points, allowing you to maintain a positive relationship with the buyer (i.e., be the good cop). Most acquisition deals involve some sort of transition period, when the seller becomes an employee of the acquirer for a certain amount of time. This can be uncomfortable if you and your new boss were hurling expletives across a negotiating table a few weeks earlier.

5. **Time the reveal.** Back in chapter 4, we talked about the slow reveal of information in a professionally run sale process. An experienced intermediary will know how to package and reveal information to keep the maximum number of acquirers interested enough to keep learning more about your company. While a lawyer may understand *what* information needs to be shared, they may not appreciate the art of knowing *how* and *when* to share it.

6. **Receive services (mostly) for free.** For all the reasons above, an experienced intermediary is likely to earn their commission a few times over by creating competition for your business and ensuring you get a fair set of deal terms. Therefore, even though they are expensive, you're probably better off financially (on a net basis) using a good intermediary.

TAKING ACTION

Realize that getting offers for your business is a "who" rather than a "how" question. Find an intermediary who knows this to help you sell your company. Start by knowing whether you need a business broker, an M&A professional, or an investment banker.

Interview a few intermediaries, and look for someone who has experience selling companies like yours and a genuine interest in what makes your business unique. Be cautious of an industry specialist if there are only a few acquirers in your industry.

As when hiring anyone that matters, check their references and make sure you like them enough personally to want to spend a lot of time together, which you'll do as you get further into selling your company.

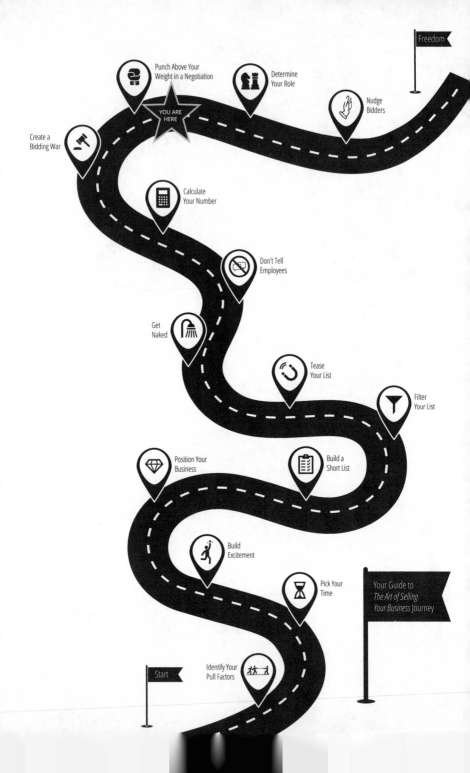

Freedom

Punch Above Your Weight in a Negotiation

YOU ARE HERE

Determine Your Role

Nudge Bidders

Create a Bidding War

Calculate Your Number

Don't Tell Employees

Get Naked

Tease Your List

Filter Your List

Position Your Business

Build a Short List

Build Excitement

Pick Your Time

Your Guide to *The Art of Selling Your Business* Journey

Start

Identify Your Pull Factors

Chapter 14

You Set the Price, I'll Set the Terms

How to Drive a Great Deal

Sunny Vanderbeck was glaring at his fax machine.

It was Friday, August 31, 2001, and as the Labor Day long weekend approached, Vanderbeck was getting nervous. Compaq had promised to fax over the paperwork confirming their acquisition offer of around $1 billion for Vanderbeck's website hosting company called Data Return.

As the hours ticked by, Vanderbeck became more restless. He picked up the receiver on the fax machine to make sure there was a dial tone. He then faxed himself a blank page to make sure the machine was still working. Every ring, beep, and buzz—the standard cacophony of sounds in a busy office—caused Vanderbeck to sprint to the fax machine, only to be disappointed as he stared at the lifeless device.

As the afternoon wore on, Vanderbeck's employees started to leave early for the weekend, but he didn't budge. Vanderbeck remained holed up in his office, waiting for the fax to arrive.

In the early evening, Vanderbeck finally decided to go home. He assured himself it must have been a technical glitch or an administrative error, and resigned himself to get to the bottom of the delay first thing after the long weekend.

Vanderbeck spent the first part of the weekend preoccupied, wondering if something had gone wrong. By Monday, as the rest of the country was celebrating a day off, Vanderbeck flipped on CNN just as the announcer described a blockbuster merger in the technology world: Compaq and HP had announced plans to merge, creating an $87 billion technology giant.

Now Vanderbeck understood why the fax had never arrived. Compaq's billion-dollar offer for his company was off the table.

This was not Vanderbeck's first disappointment in the journey of selling his company. Vanderbeck had co-founded Data Return in 1996 and grew it by 40% every quarter, leading to an initial public offering (or IPO) in 1999 and an eventual market capitalization of $3 billion.

Then the internet bubble burst.

Data Return got hit when their customers started failing and their growth flatlined. Despite the effect the market crash had on Data Return's business, Compaq still saw a lot of value in the company, which is why they were planning to buy Data Return for almost $1 billion right before their talks with HP came to a crescendo.

Immediately after the sale to Compaq was called off, Vanderbeck took stock of where his company was at. They were burning cash, and Vanderbeck figured they had six months to get a deal done before they could face mortal danger. He continued to look for a buyer and soon received another offer from a technology consulting and software business rolling up IT services companies. Vanderbeck agreed to sell Data Return in exchange for stock in the IT services rollup.

Soon after the transaction closed, Vanderbeck realized he had made a mistake. As he recounts in his book, *Selling Without Selling Out*, Vanderbeck recognized that his company's acquirer was suffering the consequences of a buying spree during which they had made 40 recent acquisitions. Data Return's acquirer had bitten off more than they could chew, and a little over a year later they declared bankruptcy.

Vanderbeck had fallen from running a company with a $3 billion market capitalization to owning shares in a bankrupt business. He still had his original Data Return partners and investors who believed in him, however, so Vanderbeck assembled his team again and bought the assets of his former company out of bankruptcy for $30 million.

Four years later, Vanderbeck sold Data Return to Terremark Worldwide in a transaction valued at $85 million. Some of that payment was made in Terremark stock, which became much more valuable over the subsequent years. "Through the many twists and turns of the Data

Return saga," Vanderbeck reflected, "I came to appreciate the terms of a deal—in particular. When a deal is considered 'done' and [the] form of payment—are just as important as the price."[43]

YOUR DEAL TERMS

If you've followed the process I've laid out so far, have a profitable business, and sprinkle in a little luck, you should start to receive offers for your company. Now comes the tricky part of negotiating the best deal you can muster.

Broadly speaking, an acquisition offer has two major components: the price and the terms by which you will get your money. Most of us focus on the acquisition price, but as Vanderbeck will tell you, the terms are arguably just as important. Are you being offered cash? Or, like Vanderbeck's first experience selling Data Return, overvalued shares of a struggling company? Will you get paid at closing or in some convoluted earnout scheme?

There's an old expression among acquirers that demonstrates the point: "You set the price, I'll set the terms." This pithy quote illustrates the importance of the terms being proposed by an acquirer, not just the headline price. In this chapter, we're going to cover a few of the crucial elements of getting you the best deal possible.

---

43   John Warrillow, "From Billion Dollar Startup to Bankruptcy and Back Again," *Built to Sell Radio*, podcast, October 4, 2019, https://builttosell.com/radio/episode-201/

YOUR LEFT TACKLE

Let's start with a quick note about a new member of your team. You are going to need an experienced M&A attorney (i.e., a lawyer) to represent you throughout the process of selling your business.

I know what you're thinking: yet another mouth to feed. True, lawyers can be pricey. But trust me—you don't want to skimp on professional advice with the most important transaction of your life. Your M&A attorney will play an important role that is slightly different from that of your intermediary.

A good lawyer's job is to protect your blind side.

As Michael Lewis points out in his book *The Blind Side*, and as was dramatized in the movie of the same name, every right-handed quarterback in football is protected by his left tackle. As the quarterback goes back in the pocket to throw, he naturally turns away from the 300-pound men trying to flatten him. The left tackle is there to ensure nobody touches the quarterback when his back is turned.

A good left tackle is one of the most sought-after players in football. They must be quick, agile, and strong. The very best also have a defensive instinct that is difficult to quantify. They see their main role as protection. They don't need to score touchdowns to feel good; they see their job as quietly enabling and protecting the guys that do.

When it comes to selling your business, a good lawyer is the equivalent of your left tackle. But just as a left tackle is probably not the guy you want to throw the ball to when it's third and long, your M&A lawyer is not the person who is going to proactively focus on getting a deal done. In fact, they will do exactly the opposite, which is another reason you need an intermediary to counterbalance the defensive stance of your lawyer.

As we covered in the previous chapter, your intermediary's posture will almost always be offensive, and their emphasis will be on getting a transaction done, because that's how they get paid. They have an interest in presenting you with acquisition offers in the best possible light and will downplay any negative terms so they can show you what a great job they're doing and get you to feel good about each offer.

Your intermediary should still be representing you by pushing for the highest possible offer and pointing out the drawbacks of each term included in an offer. But you may still feel some subtle pressure from your intermediary to accept a deal, because most of their compensation is tied to you consummating a sale with a buyer. That doesn't mean your intermediary is a bad person or an unscrupulous professional—they are simply doing their job and trying to sell your business.

Your lawyer's job is slightly different: their goal is to protect your interests in a transaction. So when it comes to scrutinizing offers, your lawyer will point out all the bad stuff. M&A lawyers often refer to terms as "market"—lawyer-speak for a clause that is reasonable and common in most acquisitions. On the contrary, terms that are overly punitive are referred to as "out of market" and should be questioned.

A lawyer and an intermediary with mutual respect for one another will act as natural counterbalancing forces. One will push for a deal; the other will pump the brakes.

An M&A attorney is a specialist who deals with buying and

selling companies. This person is a specific kind of lawyer and probably not the same attorney you hired to incorporate your business. Generalist lawyers may claim to have the expertise to represent you during the sale of your company, but that's kind of like asking your family doctor to replace your hip. A generalist lawyer may understand the basics, but M&A law is a specialty, and you need someone who does it for a living.

LETTER OF INTENT

The first document your M&A lawyer will help you review is a letter of intent. An LOI is the document most commonly used by potential acquirers to express interest in buying your company and to outline a set of proposed deal terms. It will also likely include a request for a "no-shop clause" or period of exclusivity during which you agree not to negotiate with any other buyers—something we'll visit later in this chapter.

Your LOI will include things like the price the acquirer is willing to pay, the currency they are proposing to consummate the transaction (e.g., cash, shares in their company), how they intend to calculate working capital (don't worry—we'll talk about that later in the chapter too), and usually what role they envision for you post-transaction.

If you have ever heard an entrepreneur lament that they were "just days away from selling when their deal fell apart," you were probably talking to a founder who didn't understand the difference between an LOI and a definitive purchase agreement. An LOI is usually "non-binding," meaning an acquirer can, and often does, walk away from a commitment they've made in an LOI, without penalty.[44] The LOI is the first gate you need to pass through on the way to selling your business. After the LOI is signed, you will need to endure a period of due diligence; if you survive that, you will sign a definitive purchase agreement, which is the final agreement between you and the buyer.

Part of the art of selling is to remain composed when you get your first LOI. It can be intoxicating to receive an LOI. If you are a founder who started your business from scratch, it can feel almost unbelievable that someone would pay good money for something that was simply an idea in your head a few years ago. Just like parents will always see their child as the little boy or girl they raised, a founder will always remember the early days of their business. It can seem unimaginable that your "baby" is now worth real money.

So slow down and consider the following points addressed in an LOI:

- **Offer price.** This is pretty obvious. Usually it's a number, but sometimes it can be a formula (e.g., x times EBITDA). Insist on a hard number, because a formula leaves a lot of room for interpretation after the LOI is signed.

- **Working capital calculation.** If your business is a little larger, an acquirer will usually include a proposed working capital calculation in their LOI. This formula usually takes

---

44 The one exception to this rule is a situation where an LOI is signed by both parties and includes a "breakup fee," which is an amount of money paid to the seller in the event a deal does not get done. Breakup fees are common among large company transactions but almost unheard of in smaller deals.

your accounts receivable and finished-goods inventory and subtracts your accounts payable, accrued expenses, and any short-term liabilities. Most founders consider account receivables and retained earnings as their money, whereas most buyers assume they are getting whatever working capital is in the business at the time of the offer. The working capital calculation can have a big impact on the amount of money you put in your pocket as a result of selling; take the time to work through what they're proposing with your accountant so you can be sure you understand the math.

- **Assets vs. shares.** An LOI should include a note on whether the potential acquirer is considering purchasing the assets of your company or its shares. Depending on the tax policy in your area, you will probably be better off if they purchase your shares, because most tax regimes treat the sale of shares more favorably. However, buying your shares means the acquirer is inheriting your company's liabilities, and that's why most acquirers would prefer to buy your assets instead. Here's where you'll want your accountant to show you the after-tax implications of an acquirer buying your assets versus your shares.

- **Currency.** Your LOI should include the currency the acquirer is proposing to use to buy your company. For example, are they offering you cash, shares in their company, or a combination of the two? I prefer cash because part of the reason you are likely selling is to diversify your wealth, and trading one concentrated position in a company you control for a big position in a company you don't control doesn't make a lot of sense, no matter how fast the acquirer is growing.

o You may be asked to accept some of your proceeds in shares of the acquirer's company, in which case you're going to want to understand the conditions under which you can sell those shares. Before agreeing, ask whether there is a hold-back or vesting period during which you're unable to cash in your shares.

o If your acquirer is a privately held company and they are proposing that you become a minority shareholder, you may have few (if any) options to sell your shares unless your acquirer is itself acquired.

- **Approvals.** If you receive an LOI from another company, it will sometimes allude to permissions they have received, or need to receive, in order to complete the transaction. If an LOI stipulates that the offer still needs to be approved by their board, it's less attractive than if the offer already has board approval.

- **Your role post-sale.** Your LOI will usually include a section describing the acquirer's proposed role for you post-sale. Are they asking you for terms that include an earnout scheme— that is, to earn some of your proceeds by hitting certain targets in the future? If so, what assurances are they offering that the earnout goals can be met? For a free-spirited entrepreneur, most earnouts are torture. If you will feel shackled by the con-fines of bureaucracy, my suggestion is to treat the portion of your offer locked up in an earnout as gravy: nice if you get it, but think twice before agreeing to a deal where the original cash at closing does not meet your minimum number.

- **Noncompete.** Your LOI may also propose a period of time where you will be forbidden from setting up a business similar to the one you are exiting. If you have very specific technical expertise, consider the opportunity cost of being sidelined.

- **Due diligence.** Some professional acquirers will also include a due diligence checklist of things they will need from you in order to turn their nonbinding LOI into a firm agreement to purchase your company. Expect this list to look daunting, but if you did your pre-diligence (as we discussed in chapter 3), you'll have most of this stuff on hand already.

- **Contingencies.** Often the proposed transaction will be subject to contingencies that must be achieved at or before closing to the satisfaction of the acquirer and/or the seller. Examples of typical contingencies include making the deal subject to the confirmation of financing, a favorable review of audited financial statements and tax returns, or a seller paying off all debts related to the business assets.

LOI vs. IOI

While the LOI is the most common document used to communicate an acquirer's interest in your company, instead you may get a document known as an indication of interest (IOI). While similar in purpose, an IOI is a less formal document and usually provides only a range of value (e.g., three to five times EBITDA) they might be willing to offer rather than a firm bid.

If you receive an IOI rather than an LOI, it's a sign the acquirer still needs more information to properly assess your company. So if the offer range described in the IOI meets your minimum expectations, it makes sense to explore the questions the acquirer needs to have answered in order to turn their IOI into an LOI.

HANGING ON TO YOUR LEVERAGE

Part of the art of selling is understanding when you have leverage and when you're at an acquirer's mercy. In the early stages of selling an attractive business, you have lots of leverage. Assuming you have a growing company with decent margins and a protected niche, there should be a number of companies or individuals that would like to acquire your business.

Before you sign an LOI, you are in control and can decide what you like about each offer, play one offer against the other, and—as James Murphy did so well in selling Viviscal (described in chapter 10)—ask the potential acquirers to up their bid or improve their proposed deal terms.

That leverage is significantly reduced when you sign the LOI, because almost all offers will include a no-shop clause, forcing you to terminate discussions with other potential buyers while your newfound "fiancé" does due diligence before consummating a deal. After you sign this exclusivity agreement, the balance of power in the negotiation swings heavily in favor of the buyers, who can then take their time investigating your company.

With each passing day, you will likely become more psychologically committed to selling your business. Savvy buyers know this and often drag out diligence for months, ultimately manufacturing things to justify lowering their offer price or demanding better terms in a negotiating tactic called "re-trading."

With your leverage diminished and other suitors sidelined, you're then left with the unattractive options of either accepting the inferior terms or walking away.

In one example I have firsthand knowledge of, the founder of a telecommunications equipment installer decided to sell and signed a no-shop clause as part of an LOI with a potential acquirer. The owner had built a nice business with recurring contracts driving $15 million in annual revenue and nearly $2 million in pretax profit. Instead of using an intermediary to run a professional sale process, the owner made the mistake of approaching buyers haphazardly with the help of his accountant and his lawyer.

The acquirer's due diligence dragged on for many months, culminating in the acquirer asking for concessions and delaying the process even further. The business owner had given up all his leverage; the acquirer knew he hadn't developed a set of alternative buyers before signing the no-shop clause. Finally, the deal fell apart.

Avoid this fate by negotiating any contentious elements of a deal before you sign an LOI.

LEGITIMATE VS. BAD-FAITH RE-TRADING

Re-trading can happen when something material has changed in your business during the due diligence process, or when the acquirer has discovered something bad that was not revealed to them prior to signing the LOI. This kind of re-trading is legitimate, and you open yourself up to it by letting your company's results slip during the sale process or by not being totally candid with a buyer before signing their LOI.

The other kind of re-trading is in bad faith, and it is one of the ugly truths about selling your business. There are bad actors out there who play this bait-and-switch game as a deliberate tactic. There are a few things you can do to avoid falling victim to re-trading:

- **Nail your results.** Make sure you continue to hit your numbers while you're in negotiations to sell your business. Don't give the buyer any excuses to start re-trading.

- **Be transparent.** Be truthful with acquirers in your talks leading up to receiving an LOI. Most acquirers understand no business is perfect. A professional buyer will deploy an army of analysts to find your company's trouble spots, so the truth will inevitably come out. If you're in serious talks with a potential buyer, it's worth proactively sharing things they will likely find out in diligence.

- **Check their reputation.** If you can, talk to other owners who have sold to the company whose LOI you're considering signing. Ask them about any re-trading attempts the acquirer may have made.

- **Create competition.** If an acquirer knows there are multiple buyers for a business they're interested in, they will know that re-trading could trigger you to walk away from their offer and wait out the lockout window (usually 60 or 90 days) before picking up negotiations with their competitor.

- **Limit diligence to 60 days.** After signing an LOI, the prospective acquirer will dispatch a team of analysts to validate their assumptions about your business. This process is like pulling a stray yarn on an old sweater; it will go on forever if you let it. So make sure you agree to a firm time limit on diligence with the option to restart negotiations with other acquirers if the limit is breached.

- **Use an intermediary.** An intermediary is well versed in the dark art of re-trading and will be able to call it out when it is an unscrupulous attempt to renege on an agreement.

- **Employ the no-re-trading handshake.**[45] Once you have completed your negotiations over an LOI, meet with the acquirer face-to-face. After everything has been agreed to, get up from the table and walk over to the most senior person in the room from the acquirer's side. Reach out your hand to shake theirs. Look them in the eye and say, "I'll agree to this on one condition: no re-trading. Do we have a deal?" The no-re-trading handshake works because you're telegraphing to the other side that you are a savvy seller and not likely to be fooled by a last-minute attempt at bad-faith re-trading.

---

45   Thanks to Barry Hinckley for this tip. Hinckley sold his company Bullhorn for $135 million using the no-re-trading handshake. John Warrillow, "Raising Money? Avoid This Sleazy Investor's Trap," *Built to Sell Radio*, podcast, December 7, 2016, https://builttosell.com/radio/episode-72/

TAKING ACTION

Any offer can be dressed up as attractive at first glance, so understand the deal terms—in particular, how and when you'll get your money—to properly assess it.

Hire an M&A lawyer to protect your downside as you review offers. Remember that your intermediary is likely to gently push you to close, so stand firm on the deal terms that are important to you.

Avoid countersigning an LOI with a no-shop clause until you've subtly demonstrated to an acquirer that there are other buyers pursuing you. Discuss re-trading before you sign the LOI, and make it clear you will walk at the first sign of illegitimate re-trading.

And be sure to nail your numbers during due diligence so the acquirer will not have a genuine reason to re-trade.

Freedom

Punch Above Your Weight in a Negotiation

Determine Your Role

Nudge Bidders

Create a Bidding War

YOU ARE HERE

Calculate Your Number

Don't Tell Employees

Get Naked

Tease Your List

Filter Your List

Position Your Business

Build a Short List

Build Excitement

Pick Your Time

Your Guide to *The Art of Selling Your Business* Journey

Start

Identify Your Pull Factors

Chapter 15

Earnout vs. Flameout

How to Structure Your
Role Post-Sale

In the previous chapter, we talked about negotiating deal terms, and one term is so important it warrants its own chapter: the role the acquirer wants you to play after you sell your company.

You may imagine passing the baton to a new owner like a 4 x 100 meter sprinter, but in reality, most exits are more gradual and rely on your continued involvement for a period of time after the sale. It's important to get clear on the maximum amount of two things: the time and the money you're willing to commit to help the acquirer make the most of what they have bought.

Back in chapter 3, I told you about New Zealand–based Rod Drury, who founded Aftermail to provide a better way for companies to store old emails. After roughly two years in business, and despite barely cresting $2 million in annual revenue, Aftermail was acquired by Quest Software for a reported $35 million.

The headlines in Drury's hometown newspaper trumpeted the $35 million figure, but when I interviewed Drury for my podcast, he revealed that the actual selling price was around $15 million cash with the *potential* for up to $35 million if Drury and his team met the future goals listed in his earnout contract.[46]

This was a fantastic result for a $2 million company, but Drury never saw a penny of his earnout. He estimated that he could have hit the goals had he negotiated more time. However, he underestimated the effort involved in transitioning Aftermail into another company. "It actually takes a period of time for you to embed yourself in [another company]," he explained. "We had to rebrand everything. We had to go through and do the internal selling to the [Quest] salespeople all over the world."

Drury went on to provide this advice to founders negotiating an earnout:

> If I was doing it again, while it goes against your natural instincts, I'd actually put a time delay on the earnout

---

46   John Warrillow, "The $20 Million Mistake," *Built to Sell Radio*, podcast, August 10, 2016, https://builttosell.com/radio/episode-56/

period, starting maybe three months in. In that three months you would have the opportunity [to embed yourself], and you'd be very formal about how you were going to educate all of the sales force. [I would] make sure the compensation plans for the sales force were put in place, because the timer starts right from day one, and there's a huge amount of time taken just to institutionalize a new product.

If a buyer gives you a chunk of money after months of exhausting negotiations, you will probably need a month or two to catch your breath—but you may not be able to take this break if you agreed to an earnout contract with goals you need to start hitting immediately. Often the budget you need to achieve your earnout is made available to you only if you achieve your first set of goals. Miss the first few targets, and you may trigger a domino effect that will ensure you will not meet your bogey.

Instead of obsessing over trying to reach his earnout, Drury left Quest after about a year as an employee. He took his share of the cash proceeds from the sale of Aftermail to start the wildly successful accounting software company Xero. Rather than madly trying to navigate Quest's corporate culture in an attempt to reach some ultra-stretch goal that was largely out of his control, Drury did the smart thing and left to go create something he could control.

He said later, "I never counted the earnout, to be honest. I think [you should count an] earnout as a bit of a bonus, and in hindsight, we would have maximized that. But I only ever saw Aftermail as a stepping-stone to the other things I'm doing."

At this point, you may be thinking an earnout is a bad idea. While you're right to be skeptical, it may be a mistake to be closed to the idea altogether. As a general rule, you stand to earn more money from the sale of your business if you are willing to participate in a transition period of some sort. Each of the four sections that follow describes a different role you may be asked to play, along with the pros and cons of playing that role.

I've also included examples of a typical deal where the owner enters the negotiation with hopes of a clean, 100% cash offer, but instead gets an offer that includes payments structured over time. In each hypothetical scenario, the structured payout is larger than the all-cash offer, but the guaranteed payment is lower. These examples will allow you to compare and contrast some of the more typical scenarios. Going into the process of reviewing offers, know what kind of structuring you're open to and what's a nonstarter for you.

YOUR ROLE AS LENDER (VENDOR TAKEBACK, OR VTB)

When you're selling a smaller business (less than a few million dollars in value), it's common that the buyer would get a bank loan and then ask you to finance a portion of the sale. This means instead of accepting cash for part of your proceeds, you agree to take some of your money in payments the acquirer makes to you in the future.

When the acquirer has a bank or lender providing the majority of the cash at closing, the coupon or seller note is nearly always second in line or subordinate to the buyer's lender. This means the former owner often plays the role of informal/unpaid consultant to the new owner, helping the acquirer become successful while also ensuring the security of their own future stream of payments for the purchase of the company.

Assuming you trust the buyer, you may be very happy to finance them, especially if they are willing to offer an attractive interest rate. However, it's common for buyers to ask sellers to finance a large portion of a sale; this makes it important before you start a negotiation to get clear about whether you're willing to play the role of active lender after you sell.

Example of a 20% VTB with a 5%/yr coupon over 5 years	
Sale price:	$5,000,000
Cash at closing:	$4,000,000
Portion financed over 5 years at 5%:	$1,000,000
Interest earned:	$132,274
Total potential proceeds after 5 years including interest:	**$5,132,274**

Having to finance part of your deal is very common when selling a small business, and most deals work out just fine. But as we saw in the case of David Chang (in chapter 6), VTBs can also go horribly wrong—especially when the portion of the acquisition being financed is significant.

YOUR ROLE AS DIVISION EXECUTIVE (EARNOUT)

As with Rod Drury from Aftermail, another role you may be asked to play is that of a senior leader within your acquirer's company. In this scenario, you'll be tasked with achieving a set of goals in the future in return for additional consideration for your business—an earnout, as we've discussed earlier. Acquirers use this tactic when they're buying a company that is dependent on its owner, or when they need to bridge the gap between what they are willing to pay for a business and what an owner wants.

Earnouts are especially common in service businesses or early-stage companies. They typically range between one and seven years (the average is three). Your earnout goals will likely be tied to hitting a revenue or profit target in the future, to the retention of a specific customer, or to any other objective you agree to with your buyer.

Sometimes earnouts work spectacularly well for both buyer and seller. However, there are many more examples where the owner leaves without ever realizing their earnout or suffers through a painful period as an employee of their former company. Although your lawyer will try to ensure you have the operational freedom to reach your earnout goals, new restrictions put in place by the buyer may handcuff your ability to reach those targets.

Another reason earnouts can be elusive is that the buyer—now your boss—has little incentive to help you hit your earnout objectives. Why would they help you reach your goals if it means paying millions more for them to purchase your business? In some cases, an acquirer would much prefer that you quietly realize the earnout is a mirage—and then leave, so they can get on with integrating your business into theirs.

Finally, earnouts are often tied to reaching profit goals—but you may lose your ability to manage your Profit & Loss statement when you sell your business. The buyer now controls how they choose to express your profits and what expenses they decide to allocate to your numbers. A good lawyer or intermediary will try to structure your deal so your acquirer can't arbitrarily apply expenses to your P&L post-closing, but good luck enforcing the agreement if your acquirer is a deep-pocketed giant.

In the following example, an acquirer offers to pay "up to" $7 million with a combination of cash and earnout. The up-front cash payment (known as the "downstroke" in M&A parlance) is $3 million, and the seller has the *potential* to earn an additional $4 million if they achieve their goals over a three-year earnout.

Example of a successful earnout	
Downstroke:	$3,000,000
Earnout payment:	$4,000,000
Total potential consideration:	**$7,000,000**

Keep in mind that most earnouts are not guaranteed, so drive up the value of your business so that your expectations are in line with what buyers are willing to pay, and if you are lucky enough to receive multiple offers for your company, you'll spend most of your time comparing the cash each acquirer is willing to pay at closing, because the rest may be just an illusion.

YOUR ROLE AS CONSULTANT (CONTRACT/FEE)

Another common role that a seller may be asked to play is that of consultant to the acquirer of their business. This is usually a short-term arrangement where you agree to help the new owner in return for a prearranged consulting fee.

This approach is often used when an acquirer would like to quickly integrate your business and sees only a short-term need for your help. Note that in most jurisdictions, this consulting fee will be treated as taxable income and so will likely attract the highest tax rates going. Talk to your accountant to properly compare and contrast the after-tax proceeds of any offer you get.

Let's imagine a scenario where you were hoping for a $5-million cash deal, but the acquirer offered an up-front payment of $4.8 million with a consulting contract that guarantees you $500,000 over time:

Example: A Consulting Contract	
Up-front payment:	$4,800,000
Consulting contract:	$500,000
Total potential consideration:	**$5,300,000**

If you're selling because you want to move on to a new business or project, be sure to put a time limit on the acquirer's use of your consulting time. Try to negotiate a deal that requires your consulting contract payout regardless of whether the acquirer uses the time you have allotted them.

YOUR ROLE AS SHAREHOLDER (RECAPITALIZATION)

Another role you could be asked to play is that of shareholder. In a recapitalization of your business, you sell some of your shares but usually are asked to continue to hold a significant portion of equity in your business after the investor injects money into it.

Recapitalizations are typically offered by PEGs that want to invest in your business, make it more valuable over time, and then sell their position in your company at a much higher valuation at some point in the future. Private equity companies do not usually have operational leaders on staff, so they may need you to continue running your business as both CEO and significant shareholder.

When this scheme works, you can end up earning much more from the sale of your business, because you sell the second part of your equity at a higher valuation. As mentioned in chapter 6, this is referred to by PEGs as taking a "second bite of the apple."

As in an earnout, in a recapitalization you sell only part of your equity. You continue to risk some of your wealth in the business, because it's possible your equity will become worthless if the company fails after the recapitalization.

In the hypothetical scenario below, the owner was hoping for an all-cash offer of $5 million but was offered $3 million in cash for 60% of their business with a *chance* at selling the second tranche of their equity at a much higher valuation within three to seven years.

Example: A successful recapitalization	
Sell 60% of your shares:	$3,000,000
Sell the remaining 40% seven years later:	$7,000,000
Total potential consideration:	**$10,000,000**

Most recapitalizations are fueled by debt the private equity company uses to ratchet up its return on investing in your business. In some sleazy cases, the PEG tries to name you as a guarantor of the debt they are taking on to buy your business; this is a little like selling your house and then co-signing the borrower's mortgage. Have your lawyer vet any recapitalization offers to ensure you're not on the hook for the debt the investor is taking on to acquire or grow your business.

TAKING ACTION

There are many different ways to structure your role after the sale of your business, and the categories discussed in this chapter represent examples of the most common transaction types. Part of the art of selling is to remain open to the benefits of all deal structures rather than becoming too fixated on just one of them.

The more flexible you seem before signing an LOI, the more offers you are likely to attract. In an ironic twist, by encouraging more offers, your flexibility puts you in a better position to dictate the role you want to play post-exit.

The opposite is not true. If you are too rigid and appear unwilling to help the new owner integrate what they are considering acquiring, you are likely to turn off a lot of buyers. As a result, you'll undermine your negotiating leverage.

Stay open to all sorts of roles in order to attract the widest possible set of offers, and you'll be in the best position to negotiate the role you really want.

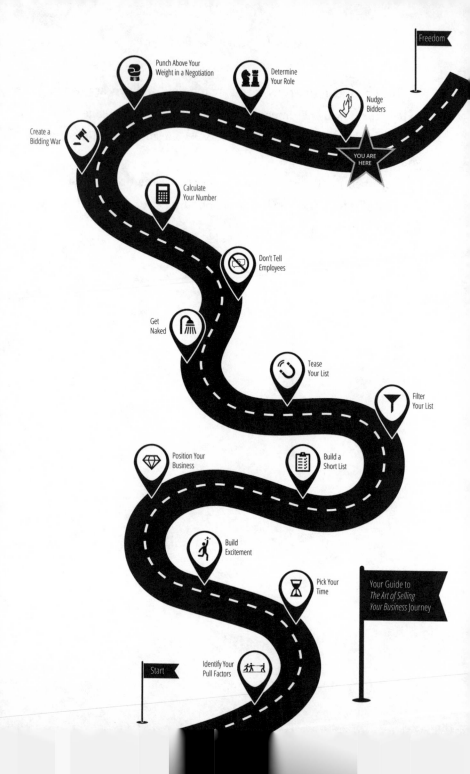

Freedom

Punch Above Your
Weight in a Negotiation

Determine
Your Role

Nudge
Bidders

Create a
Bidding War

YOU ARE
HERE

Calculate
Your Number

Don't Tell
Employees

Get
Naked

Tease
Your List

Filter
Your List

Position Your
Business

Build a
Short List

Build
Excitement

Pick Your
Time

Your Guide to
*The Art of Selling
Your Business* Journey

Start

Identify Your
Pull Factors

Chapter 16

THE ART OF THE NUDGE

HOW TO (GENTLY) SQUEEZE AN
ACQUIRER FOR MORE

Stephanie Breedlove was on hold.

Again.

It was the third time her call had been transferred, and she was getting fed up. Cradling her infant son in one arm, she lodged the phone between her ear and shoulder as she fumbled to find yet another document that was required.

An associate on the fast track to become a partner at Andersen Consulting, the predecessor to Accenture, Breedlove thought her task was simple enough: she wanted to pay the nanny she had just hired to care for her son. She had called one of the giant payroll providers, but they had shown little interest in setting up a new account to pay just one employee. The payroll company was, after all, in an industry that makes only a tiny margin on each paycheck it issues.

At dinner that night, Breedlove recounted the story to her husband, a rising star at Ernst & Young. As she described the frustration of having her call transferred to multiple agents, each one less interested than the last in helping her, she had an idea. What if she set up a payroll company just for parents to pay their nannies?

The concept was simple enough. By focusing on parents with nannies to pay, Breedlove could master the process of setting up a new account. Paying a caregiver requires a parent to complete a batch of confusing government forms. If Breedlove could simplify the process, she figured she could make a reasonable profit from busy parents who didn't have the time to navigate a labyrinth of state and federal government departments.

Breedlove & Associates was born.

After 20 years in business, Breedlove & Associates was profitably generating $9 million in annual revenue from a customer base of 10,000 parents. Breedlove's two sons were all grown up, and she was beginning to consider what was next for her and her husband, who had also left a corporate career to join his wife's business.

When Breedlove considered the landscape of companies that could benefit from the business she had built, one strategic acquirer immediately stood out. Care.com was creating an online marketplace of local care providers and had amassed seven million subscribers— mostly people with a need to hire a nanny or an elder care worker.

The concept was similar to an Angie's List for care providers. Parents could visit Care.com, type in their address, and immediately receive a list of local nannies rated by other parents who had entrusted the site with helping them find a caregiver for their child. The company had recently raised a significant round of venture capital and was looking to expand quickly.

Breedlove & Associates began with a simple marketing partnership that provided content for Care.com's seven million subscribers. After the smaller company had spent a few months delivering content and developing relationships with the Care.com team, Sheila Marcelo, founder and CEO of Care.com, reached out to explore a deeper partnership.

Marcelo immediately saw the potential of acquiring the payroll company, and a few weeks later she presented Breedlove with an offer to buy her business for $39 million. To put that number into perspective, a typical service business in the United States may hope to garner one times its annual revenue. Here was Breedlove being offered more than *four* times that amount.

Most owners would have jumped at Marcelo's offer, but Breedlove demurred, believing Marcelo would pay more given the synergies between the two companies. Breedlove showed Marcelo how she had built a profitable $9 million company with 10,000 customers. She reasoned that if just 1% of Care.com's seven million subscribers were to buy Breedlove's payroll service, it would create a company seven times the size of Breedlove & Associates almost overnight.

Just six weeks later, Marcelo upped her bid to $54 million in cash and Care.com stock. Breedlove, having negotiated a price equivalent to *six* times her annual revenue, agreed to the acquisition.[47]

Breedlove didn't just ask for an extra $15 million; she made a quantitative case about the strategic value of owning her company. And it paid off.

Getting the Best Deal Possible

At this point in the process, hopefully you're considering multiple offers from acquirers. Even if you have received only one offer, you have played the game and given an acquirer the *illusion* that there are other bidders at the table.

This chapter provides some negotiating tactics designed to ensure you get the best deal possible. Our goal is to get any potential acquirers to improve their offer or deal terms. At the very least, by carefully nudging an acquirer to increase their offer, you'll sleep better at night after the sale, knowing you did everything you could to maximize your take.

As with any negotiation, you'll drive a tougher bargain if you're willing to walk away, but bluffing can backfire unless you have a lot of attractive offers. Believe it or not, your would-be acquirer will probably get on just fine without buying your business. Unless you have something absolutely irresistible (go ahead and assume you don't), an acquirer pushed too hard may walk—leaving you with nothing.

---

47 John Warrillow, "Would You Have the Audacity to Turn Down $40MM for a $9MM Company?," *Built to Sell Radio*, podcast, December 21, 2016, https://builttosell.com/radio/episode-74/

To get an acquirer to increase their offer, you have to find the middle ground between expressing gratitude for a firm bid—they've probably already done a lot of work to get to that point—and nudging them gently to do better. The more offers you have, the harder you can push. It's not easy to achieve this delicate balance, but here are some useful tactics you can try.

CLARIFY YOUR BATNA

First, you need to get clear on your best alternative to a negotiated agreement (BATNA)—in other words, your plan B. The stronger your BATNA, the more leverage you have over an acquirer.

Your BATNA could be an offer from a PEG to recapitalize your company. Or perhaps it could be a plan to sell the company to your management team, or a willingness to keep running your business rather than selling it. The happier you are to hold on to your business, the more leverage you have in a negotiation.

If you are willing to continue operating your business, you already have at least one offer for your company. Each day you continue to own and operate your business independently, you're effectively telling the market that you would rather own your shares than sell them at the market rate and invest the proceeds in something else.

Therefore, you already have a standing offer to buy your business, so I give you permission to let an acquirer know they are already competing with at least one other bidder—they just don't need to know the one making the other offer is you.

Provided you're comfortable with your BATNA, one approach to driving a better deal is to simply ask. Let the prospective acquirer know that, compared with the other offer on the table, theirs is a little light. Explain how excited you are about the synergies between the two of you, and let them know they'll need to do a little better if they want to acquire your business.

As we talked about in chapter 10, which described James Murphy's sale of Viviscal, you can be confident when you ask for more if you have a large, attractive business with multiple bidders at the table.

But what if you have a smaller company with only one or two interested acquirers? Before they can increase their offer, an acquirer will need to go back and ask their stakeholders (their boss, board, or investment committee) to approve a higher bid. For that to be successful, you need to give them ammunition.

Sometimes, an individual executive representing an acquirer may personally want to increase their offer, but may be handcuffed by their board and therefore able to offer only what the board has approved. In this case, you have to—figuratively speaking—get up from the table and move over to the acquirer's side. Imagine you're on the same team and the two of you just want to find a way to get a deal done together. Ask the acquirer what they think about valuation. Ask what synergies they considered in developing their bid and what nonnegotiable limitations they are up against.

For example, an acquirer may have board approval to bid on companies up to a predetermined multiple of earnings. They may also have lending covenants, which limit the multiple of earnings they can pay for a business. Give the acquirer the ammunition they need to make the case to their stakeholders about why they should go beyond their normal acquisition parameters.

APPLY THE MAGIC OF ADJUSTMENTS

Remember that while an acquirer may not be able to exceed a specific multiple, you may still be in a position to increase the absolute dollar amount of their bid by focusing on the profit they are multiplying. This involves a process M&A professionals refer to as "normalizing," "recasting," or "adjusting" your P&L.[48]

The process of adjusting a P&L sounds nefarious, but it isn't if it's done professionally. The practice involves expressing your P&L so that it is the most accurate representation of the likely performance of your business in the hands of an acquirer.

For example, if you pay yourself $200,000 per year, yet an acquirer could replace you with a general manager with an annual salary of $120,000, you could recast the executive compensation expense on your P&L from $200,000 to $120,000, thereby increasing your profitability on an adjusted basis by $80,000.

There may be other things you expense to your business that an acquirer wouldn't need to pay. For example, if you are in the habit of charging your company for your annual vacation by claiming it as a business trip (don't worry—I won't tell), you could remove this expense from your P&L, which will have the effect of increasing your profit by the same amount.[49]

---

48 In a very small business, your broker will attempt to arrive at seller's discretionary earnings, or SDE, which involves a similar although not identical set of calculations.

49 Be careful running excessive personal expenses through your company. Use your company as a personal piggy bank for too long, and a banker or buyer may take the position that these expenses are in fact normal and will push back against your attempts to recast them out of your expenses.

Other typical adjustments you may be able to make include expenses associated with the following:

- A one-off lawsuit (litigation)

- Moving your location

- Excess (not strictly business-related) entertainment and travel

- Rent higher than the market rate

- Special or one-off donations

- Key man life insurance premiums

This is not an exhaustive list, and adjustments can work the other way. A buyer may argue that you need to account for additional expenses. A good intermediary will help you come up with an adjusted P&L statement you can defend.

HOW ARI ACKERMAN GOT HIS NUMBER

Ari Ackerman knows all about adjustments. He started Bunk1 in 1999 to give parents a method to keep in touch with their kids at summer camp. Bunk1's one-way window provides parents access to photo galleries, newsletters, and videos, and lets them send printed notes to their campers.

Over 17 years, Ackerman grew his technology business into one of the biggest brands in the summer camp industry. Then he was approached by Togetherwork, a company backed by a billion-dollar private equity giant.

Togetherwork told Ackerman they would be willing to pay around seven times EBITDA for Bunk1, but Ackerman wasn't satisfied. "I looked at the number and said I'm sorry, this just isn't enough for what I've built over the last 18 years," he said.

And he wasn't just thinking about himself. "It's really everybody that has helped build the company to where it is. It just didn't feel right," he continued. "It just wasn't the offer [where] I thought I could say, 'Okay, I'm turning my baby over to you, and this is something that's fair.'"[50]

Trying to bridge the gap between what he wanted for Bunk1 and what Togetherwork could pay, Ackerman set about the normalization process and projected what Bunk1's profit would be in Togetherwork's hands.

"We ended up coming up with a really interesting approach in that we used the trailing 12 months revenue number, but then we did an adjusted expense number," Ackerman explained. "We took out expenses [to show] if we were acquired by Togetherwork, what expenses wouldn't be there anymore—and they took out those expenses to the point where it became a very attractive net profit number, and the multiple of that profit number was then a much more palatable number in terms of selling Bunk1."

In the end, Togetherwork increased its bid to a point where Ackerman was willing to accept it—not because they were suddenly willing to pay a higher multiple for Bunk1, but because the number they were multiplying had increased as a result of the adjustments process.

---

50 John Warrillow, "How EBITDA Adjustments Impact the Value of Your Business," *Built to Sell Radio*, podcast, June 14, 2017, https://builttosell.com/radio/episode-96/

QUANTIFY THE ACQUIRER'S UPSIDE

Another way you can attempt to get an acquirer to increase their offer is to quantify how they will benefit from buying your business. This is a process the acquirer will do on their own, but based on the knowledge you have of your company and industry, you may be in a better spot to point out other synergies they may not have thought of.

Your goal should be to make a rational argument that quantifies the money the acquirer stands to make by owning your company. To begin, you likely can show them that their acquisition will be "accretive"—M&A lingo to describe an acquisition that increases the value of the acquirer's business.

Let's imagine a publicly traded company is trading for 10 times EBITDA when they pay $7 million of their cash to buy a company generating $1 million. They paid seven times EBITDA (7 x $1,000,000 = $7,000,000). But when they express that $1 million worth of profit on *their* P&L, it will give them a $10 million bump in valuation because their stock trades at 10 x EBITDA. Provided their stock doesn't trade down on the news of the acquisition (unlikely for a small deal), they would increase the value of their company by $3 million—without lifting a finger!

Now imagine the acquirer makes the same acquisition and instead of paying $7 million in cash, they borrow most of the money to buy your business. Suddenly the deal is exponentially more accretive.

Since bigger companies usually trade at higher multiples than smaller ones, your deal will likely be accretive for the acquirer. Go further and do your best to quantify all the other ways the acquirer will increase the value of their business by owning yours.

DEMONSTRATE HOW YOUR COMPANY WILL SELL MORE OF *THEIR* STUFF

Stephanie Breedlove did a great job of showing how Care.com could sell their subscribers her payroll service. Showing an acquirer how owning your company will give them a new product or service to sell is a great start, but the master negotiator goes further to describe how buying your company will help the acquirer sell more of *their* product or service.

As owners, we can be forgiven for looking at our world through blinders. If you're like most founders, for years you've been focused on developing your company and selling your products and services. This focus has the tendency to leave us seeing the world through the lens of our business, which is a mistake when it comes to selling it.

Your goal should be to understand what your acquirer is trying to achieve and to show them how owning your business helps them accomplish their goal. Remember, the acquirer is just as myopic as you are about your company; they will react more favorably if you can show them how owning your company helps them sell more of *their* product.

QUANTIFY YOUR VALUE

Refer back to chapter 7, when we talked about the strategic premium some buyers will pay to acquire your business. As described earlier, some of the most common reasons businesses make acquisitions are to give them the following:

- A point of differentiation for their marketing

- A leg up in competing with their archenemy
- A big enough share of the market to control the price of a key product or service
- Access to a new market
- A way to save money
- A new list of customers for their product
- A way to improve margins through volume discounts or rebates from their suppliers

At this point, you need to fire up a spreadsheet and attempt to *quantify* the strategic value of owning your business. Show an acquirer your math, and run scenarios that demonstrate how— even in the worst case—they will make out like bandits by buying your business.

An acquirer will take the position that the strategic premium is theirs to enjoy entirely and has nothing to do with you. Your job is to nudge them gently to give up a small slice. Remember, if your acquirer is five to 20 times the size of your company (as discussed in chapter 8), and if they have a solid reason to buy your business, a sliver of the strategic premium could amount to a big bonus for you.

KILL THEM WITH KINDNESS

One final word on maximizing any offer you get: no matter how low an offer is, try to work with it.

When you get a low-ball offer, you may feel a wave of righteous indignation rise up from your belly. You may find yourself cursing a prospective acquirer under your breath, enraged by how little they respect what you've built.

Let your emotions boil, but don't reveal your disgust to the buyer. The art of selling well is to take any offer—no matter how low—and try to nudge it up.

Just ask Gary Miller what being patient with an acquirer can do for the outcome of a negotiation. As mentioned earlier, Miller founded Aragon Consulting Group as a project-based professional services firm. Like most consultants, Aragon started out hawking hours. They sold their partners' time and won some big-name clients.

As the company grew, Aragon began to specialize in analyzing data and built proprietary tools that allowed clients to simulate the market adoption of their latest products and even predict the likely reaction of their competitors.

It was the early days of artificial intelligence, and Aragon won the attention of some big-name clients including IBM, which loved the company so much that they asked Aragon if they could license the technology to leverage for their own consulting clients.

Miller was hesitant.

He knew licensing the technology to IBM was risky. Miller thought that once the data scientists at IBM got under the hood of his algorithms, it could be difficult to enforce Aragon's ownership of its intellectual property (IP). While he could try to protect the model they had built, he didn't think he could win an IP infringement argument against deep-pocketed IBM.

IBM countered, guaranteeing Aragon $20 million a year in annual licensing revenue. Again, Miller demurred.

"In any of their contracts, most companies always have an

out," Miller said when I interviewed him on *Built to Sell Radio*. He continued:

> So we thought, *We're just better off selling them the company if they [want our IP],* or *We'll take this technology to HP or McKinsey or any number of other consulting companies.* [IBM] knew that those were our options, so it didn't leave them a lot of choice. They either had to buy it, or they had to build it themselves—because they tried the partnering route in any number of ways, and we just said no to partnering: *Either buy us, or you can go build it yourself.*[51]

Finally, IBM agreed to make an acquisition offer. At the time, Aragon had grown to 153 employees. Given the success of their predictive modeling product and their growth, Miller was quietly hoping for an offer of eight times EBITDA, which is why he was so disappointed to get IBM's initial offer: just three times EBITDA for Aragon's assets.

IBM's offer, said Miller, "was pretty poor for a number of reasons. We thought that [our] technology had a lot more power to it and, therefore, would gain more revenue for IBM or anybody else that would use it. We didn't think that three times EBITDA was adequate compensation for what we thought the long-term stretch was for the technology we'd invented. That was number one.

---

51   John Warrillow, "How to Handle a Low-Ball Offer," *Built to Sell Radio*, podcast, January 4, 2019, https://builttosell.com/radio/episode-163/

"Number two, they wanted to make an asset purchase. We then would have been taxed at ordinary income [rates] as opposed to a stock sale, which we would have been taxed as long-term capital gains."[52] Instead of revealing his disappointment, Miller played nice.

> The first thing I did was thank them for their offer. I told them how much we appreciated their offer and the thoughtfulness that they had put into it. However, I said, the problem with the offer is that we're going to be taxed at the level that we just don't feel we need to be taxed, since we're a C-corp. We want to be able to offset those taxes. If you want an asset sale, then the price is going to have to go up significantly to pay for the tax liability that we are all going to have as partners of the firm.

Miller kept a cool head and avoided the temptation to reveal his irritation at the buyer's low-ball offer. Here's what he had to say about that:

> It never, ever works—at least that I've seen—if you start to get angry over things. That's where business owners make such big mistakes. They are so emotionally involved. In this case, we as partners treated this just like any other transaction that we would have with our clients. You're courteous. You're nice, but you're firm. You support (your case) with rational facts.

---

52 Talk to your accountant about the pros and cons of an asset sale versus a stock sale in your area.

Instead of countering IBM's offer to purchase his assets for three times EBITDA, Miller simply asked IBM to reconsider their offer. "I just asked them to revisit the issues," he said, "and relook at the quality of the company, the bench strength of the company, our pipeline of business, and who our clients were, and see if they may have erred on the side of a low offer."

Miller described what happened next:

> They went back and modeled among themselves how much revenue they could generate from our predictive modeling technology among their existing clients. Second, [they realized] this was a vehicle for them to expand their touch points within their major companies. They would no longer be limited to the CIO. They could go to the CMO, as an example—the chief marketing officer. They could go to the CFO with various scenarios . . . we opened up the C-suite for them [with] this product.

Shortly after, IBM came back and agreed to make their acquisition a stock purchase, offering 8.5 times EBITDA for Aragon.

Miller, having moved IBM past his original goal, pushed even further. He thanked IBM for their offer again but suggested that instead of valuing Aragon by a multiple of earnings, IBM should consider using a multiple of *revenue*. Miller suggested 1.5 times annual revenue. Ultimately IBM agreed to 1.2 times revenue, or approximately 11 times EBITDA.

Miller had almost quadrupled IBM's original offer. Not once did he raise his voice, pound his fist on the table, or throw a fit. He simply stayed calm and made the case to the acquirer as to why they should pay more. And his patience paid off.

TAKING ACTION

The art of getting an acquirer to increase their offer is a delicate dance. Overplay your hand, and they may walk. You have to find the middle ground, expressing gratitude for their offer while nudging them to improve it. The more potential buyers you have bidding, the bolder you can be in asking for more.

Adjust your P&L to show how much more profit your company will generate in an acquirer's hands.

Quantify their upside.

No matter how offended you are by a low-ball offer, stay calm and see if you can gently nudge it up. Even with just one offer, you may be able to improve it by making a rational argument that helps the acquirer quantify the strategic value of owning your company.

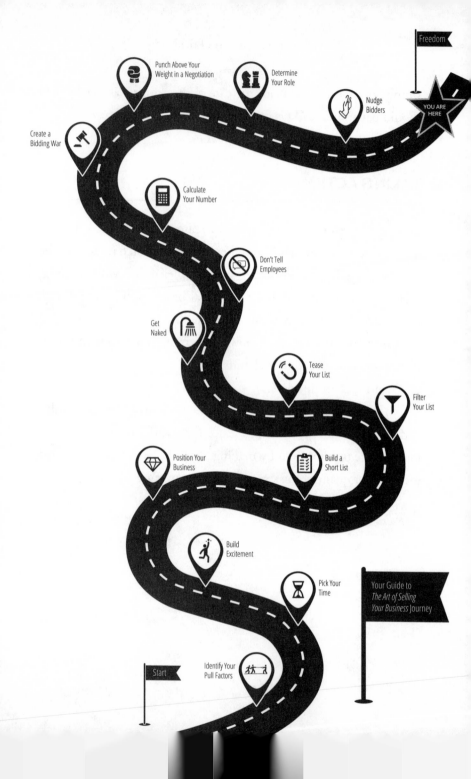

Freedom

Punch Above Your Weight in a Negotiation

Determine Your Role

Nudge Bidders

YOU ARE HERE

Create a Bidding War

Calculate Your Number

Don't Tell Employees

Get Naked

Tease Your List

Filter Your List

Position Your Business

Build a Short List

Build Excitement

Pick Your Time

Your Guide to
*The Art of Selling
Your Business* Journey

Start

Identify Your Pull Factors

Chapter 17

THE FREEDOM PARADOX

HOW TO GET COMFORTABLE WITH YOUR DECISION TO SELL

"So *you're* the douchebag who wrote *Built to Sell*."

It was the opening line from a podcaster interviewing me about my 2011 book on building company value.

That insult put me on the defensive.

The interviewer was making the point that the very best companies are built for the long-term, and only the greediest, most merciless founders build to sell.

I don't know how well I rebutted his criticism that day, but his comment had me reflect on the pervasive attitude that exists today: selling your business is akin to selling out.

Respectfully, I disagree.

Starting a business is not a life sentence. Nowhere is it written that you have to own it forever. One of the most common things I hear from founders on my podcast is: "I wish I'd done it sooner."

Often, we start a business for the sense of freedom we hope it will give us. Early in your company's life cycle, you have all the freedom you want and can decide how and where you will work.

As it grows over time, your business starts to chip away at that freedom, and you can start to feel imprisoned—both financially and psychologically—by what you've created. Not only might you feel trapped by your business, but *it* might feel confined by *you* too.

THE BOB DYLAN EFFECT

As the lyrics in Bob Dylan's song "Like a Rolling Stone" reference, when you've got nothing, then you don't have anything to lose. When you started your business, it was probably next to worthless, so it was a negligible part of your net worth. If your company has grown, it is now a larger share of your overall wealth, so it's natural to become more risk averse as you expand.

That's exactly when you go from your company's biggest driver to its main drag.

Just ask Joey Redner how it feels when your business keeps asking you to double down. Redner started his career in Tampa Bay as a sales representative for a brewery and wrote a column about beer for the local newspaper. At night he brewed small batches at home.

In 2007, Redner noticed something strange. Of the beer sold in the United States, 10% was now bought from small craft brewers, but just 2% of Tampa beer came from the little guys. Redner decided Tampa needed its own craft brewer and set out to create what would become Cigar City Brewing.

Redner estimated he would need $850,000 to buy the equipment to brew beer commercially, so he invested all of his savings and borrowed the rest from his father.

Cigar City sold 1,000 barrels of beer in their first year, and Redner realized he could have sold more had his operations been able to handle it. He offered to roll his father's remaining debt into equity and took out a small business administration (SBA) loan to add capacity.

Cigar City kept growing as fast as Redner could add volume. By 2016, Redner was up to 50,000 barrels a year on the backs of 70 full-time employees. Redner had started Cigar City as a simple extension of a hobby, and it was now among the 15 largest craft brewers in the country.

But all was not well in Tampa.

Redner had reached capacity on his facilities and needed to expand again. He had yet to pay off his SBA loan, and now he estimated he would need $20 million to build enough brewing capacity to keep up with demand. Redner couldn't stomach the stress of doubling down yet again. He described the situation this way:

> I just personally couldn't get my head around being that far in debt. I felt like I put my chips on the table, I won the bet, and then the dealer is saying, *Well, not only do you have to leave your winnings on the table, but you have to leave your original bet on the table. Oh, and by the way, you have to match both of those things.* I just felt like

my success was actually leading me to being more enslaved instead of more free. Because while [the business is] successful, [and] it's doing well, the market forces are telling me that I have to go into more debt. It just didn't make sense to me.

I wanted to be free. I wanted to be in a situation where if the business doesn't do well, I'm not beholden to write a check to someone to pay back the equipment that I bought, hoping the business would do well. That's really what pushed me ultimately in the direction of selling.[53]

In March 2016, private-equity-backed Oskar Blues announced they had acquired Cigar City Brewing. Redner was finally free.

Not only was Redner financially free, but he was also free of the stress that comes from running a business that makes up the bulk of your wealth. This tension can take a psychological toll.

When I asked Tim Ferriss why he sold his supplements company BrainQUICKEN, which had become the inspiration for *The Four-Hour Workweek*, he told me the reason wasn't the stress of running the business. Instead, it was the mental drain of always thinking about the business. "My brain felt like a computer running antivirus software in the background," he said. "Even though the company didn't take much time to run, it was consuming more than 10% of my mental energy."[54]

Selling your business is the natural culmination of a job well

---

53 John Warrillow, "How Cigar City Brewing Got Oskar Blues To Triple Their Acquisition Offer," *Built to Sell Radio*, podcast, June 21, 2017, https://builttosell.com/radio/episode-97/

54 John Warrillow, "Why Tim Ferriss Sold His Muse," *Inc.*, November 11, 2010, https://www.inc.com/articles/2010/10/why-tim-ferriss-sold-brainquicken.html

done. It means you have conceived of an idea, built it to be independent of you, and then set it free to thrive on its own. A founder who keeps their company beyond a certain point is akin to a parent who can't let go. There comes a time when your kids need to leave the house in order to reach their potential—and the same is true of your business.

It's hard for most of us to recognize that spot. It's natural to think your business still needs you—or you need it. But there may be someone else out there who is better suited to running your company now. Founders thrive on solving problems. A premium is placed on your creativity in the early years. As your business grows, however, a new set of skills are required—ones you may not have or care to learn.

It's okay to sell your business. You're not a cop-out or a sellout. In fact, you're just the opposite. You want your business to succeed on its own and—as hard as it feels some days—you know letting someone else take a turn running it may be the best thing for it.

When you started your business, you were free. I hope this book has given you a road map for getting that feeling back again.

ACKNOWLEDGMENTS

First, thank you to all of the *Built to Sell Radio* guests who have given their time and shared their experiences—sometimes in painful detail—with our community. They are:

Tina Youngblood, CEO, Pathfinder Health
Show date: January 31, 2020
https://builttosell.com/radio/episode-215/

Scott Raymond, Founder, Raymond Property Management
Show date: January 10, 2020
https://builttosell.com/radio/episode-214/

Wes Winham Founder, PolicyStat
Show date: January 3, 2020
https://builttosell.com/radio/episode-213/

Marc-Andre Seguin, Founder, JazzGuitarLessons.net
Show date: December 20, 2019
https://builttosell.com/radio/episode-212/

David Bach Founder, PlatypusNeuro
Show date: December 13, 2019
https://builttosell.com/radio/episode-211/

Zain Hasan, Founder, National Insurance Consulting Group
Show date: December 6, 2019
https://builttosell.com/radio/episode-210/

Jean-Eric Plamondon, Founder, Prairie Metal Recycling
Show date: November 29, 2019
https://builttosell.com/radio/episode-209/

Michael Houlihan, Founder, Barefoot Wines
Show date: November 22, 2019
https://builttosell.com/radio/episode-208/

Bonnie Harvey, Founder, Barefoot Wines
Show date: November 22, 2019
https://builttosell.com/radio/episode-208/

Alex McClafferty, Founder, WP Curve
Show date: November 15, 2019
https://builttosell.com/radio/episode-206/

Sherry Deutschmann, Founder, LetterLogic
Show date: November 8, 2019
https://builttosell.com/radio/episode-205/

Ian Silverberg, Founder, Silverline Ventures
Show date: October 25, 2019
https://builttosell.com/radio/episode-204/

Arik Levy, Founder, Luxer One
Show date: October 18, 2019
https://builttosell.com/radio/episode-203/

Tom Pisello, Founder, Alinean
Show date: October 11, 2019
https://builttosell.com/radio/episode-202/

Sunny Vanderbeck, Founder, Data Return
Show date: October 4, 2019
https://builttosell.com/radio/episode-201/

Timothy O'Neill-Dunne, Founder, Air Black Box
Show date: September 27, 2019
https://builttosell.com/radio/episode-200/

Peter Kelly, Founder, OPENLANE
Show date: September 20, 2019
https://builttosell.com/radio/episode-199/

Mark Deutschmann, Founder, Village Real Estate
Show date: September 13, 2019
https://builttosell.com/radio/episode-198/

Glenn Grant, Founder, G2 Technology
Show date: September 6, 2019
https://builttosell.com/radio/episode-197/

David Heimlich, Founder, Nation Leagues
Show date: August 29, 2019
https://builttosell.com/radio/episode-196/

Tommy Berretz, Founder, Texas Aquatic Enterprises
Show date: August 23, 2019
https://builttosell.com/radio/episode-195/

John MacInnes, Founder, Print Audit
Show date: August 16, 2019
https://builttosell.com/radio/episode-194/

Dinesh Dhamija, Founder, eBookers.com
Show date: August 9, 2019
https://builttosell.com/radio/episode-193/

Matt Slaine, Founder, Progressive Business Media
Show date: August 2, 2019
https://builttosell.com/radio/episode-192/

James Roman, Founder, iVelocity
Show date: July 26, 2019
https://builttosell.com/radio/episode-191/

Matt Darby, Founder, Matched Pattern
Show date: July 19, 2019
https://builttosell.com/radio/episode-190/

Kristin Delwo, Founder, Stacks
Show date: July 12, 2019
https://builttosell.com/radio/episode-189/

Lori Moen, Owner, Viking Trophies
Show date: July 5, 2019
https://builttosell.com/radio/episode-188/

Aurangzeb Khan, Founder, Altia Systems
Show date: June 28, 2019
https://builttosell.com/radio/episode-187/

Ken Kramer, President, TerrAlign
Show date: June 21, 2019
https://builttosell.com/radio/episode-186/

Jessica Tindel, Founder, Dream Enrichment Classes
Show date: June 7, 2019
https://builttosell.com/radio/episode-185/

Wayne Colonna, Owner, Automatic Transmission Support Group
Show date: May 31, 2019
https://builttosell.com/radio/episode-184/

Ryan Deiss, Founder, Traffic & Conversion Summit
Show date: May 24, 2019
https://builttosell.com/radio/episode-183/

CJ Whelan, Founder, Adigo
Show date: May 17, 2019
https://builttosell.com/radio/episode-182/

Alex Bates, Founder, Mtell
Show date: May 10, 2019
https://builttosell.com/radio/episode-181/

Acknowledgments

Andrew Lamppa, Owner, 44th Street Diner
Show date: May 3, 2019
https://builttosell.com/radio/episode-180/

Boyd Davis, Founder, Kogentix
Show date: April 26, 2019
https://builttosell.com/radio/episode-179/

Erik Van Horn, Franchise Owner, Sola Salon Studios
Show date: April 12, 2019
https://builttosell.com/radio/episode-178/

Kenan Hopkins, Founder, Blue Ridge To Go
Show date: April 5, 2019
https://builttosell.com/radio/episode-177/

Jonathon Moody, Founder, Versature
Show date: March 29, 2019
https://builttosell.com/radio/episode-176/

Ross Buhrdorf, Co-Founder, HomeAway
Show date: March 22, 2019
https://builttosell.com/radio/episode-175/

Connie Fenyo, Owner, Dye & Durham
Show date: March 15, 2019
https://builttosell.com/radio/episode-174/

Drew Kraemer, Founder, Marketplace Strategy
Show date: March 8, 2019
https://builttosell.com/radio/episode-173-2/

Rob Daly, Co-Founder, Stelligent
Show date: March 1, 2019
https://builttosell.com/radio/episode-173/

Paul Duvall, Co-Founder, Stelligent
Show date: March 1, 2019
https://builttosell.com/radio/episode-173/

Ann Bennett, Founder, Applied Information Services
Show date: February 22, 2019
https://builttosell.com/radio/episode-171/

Mitch Durfee, Founder, Grunts Move Junk
Show date: February 15, 2019
https://builttosell.com/radio/episode-170/

Mitchell Reichgut, Founder, Jun Group
Show date: February 8, 2019
https://builttosell.com/radio/episode-169/

Rand Fishkin, Founder, Moz
Show date: February 4, 2019
https://builttosell.com/radio/episode-168/

John Dalton, Founder, Industrial Device Investments
Show date: February 1, 2019
https://builttosell.com/radio/episode-167/

Judith Nowlin, Founder, iBirth
Show date: January 18, 2019
https://builttosell.com/radio/episode-166/

Kimberly Caccavo, Founder, GRACEDBYGRIT
Show date: January 11, 2019
https://builttosell.com/radio/episode-165/

Kate Nowlan, Founder, GRACEDBYGRIT
Show date: January 11, 2019
https://builttosell.com/radio/episode-165/

Gary Miller, Founder, Aragon Consulting
Show date: January 4, 2019
https://builttosell.com/radio/episode-163/

Philip Williams, Founder, hydroGEOPHYSICS
Show date: December 14, 2018
https://builttosell.com/radio/episode-162/

Acknowledgments

Brandon Neth, Founder, Northwest Cannabis Solutions
Show date: December 7, 2018
https://builttosell.com/radio/episode-161/

Tyler Tringas, Founder, Storemapper
Show date: November 30, 2018
https://builttosell.com/radio/episode-160/

Carl Allen, Editor, Dealmaker Wealth Society
Show date: November 23, 2018
https://builttosell.com/radio/episode-159/

Steve Murch, Founder, VacationSpot.com
Show date: November 2, 2018
https://builttosell.com/radio/episode-158/

Keith Weigand, Founder, DataNet Solutions
Show date: October 26, 2018
https://builttosell.com/radio/episode-157/

Mark Janes, Founder, ConnectedYard
Show date: October 19, 2018
https://builttosell.com/radio/episode-156/

Diana House, Founder, Tiny Devotions
Show date: October 12, 2018
https://builttosell.com/radio/episode-155/

Peter Fader, Founder, Zodiac
Show date: October 5, 2018
https://builttosell.com/radio/episode-154/

George Bandarian II, Owner, AMI
Show date: September 28, 2018
https://builttosell.com/radio/episode-153/

Angela Mader, Founder, fitlosophy
Show date: September 21, 2018
https://builttosell.com/radio/episode-152/

Jim Remsik, Founder, Adorable
Show date: September 14, 2018
https://builttosell.com/radio/episode-151/

Mitchell Feldman, Founder, Cloudamour
Show date: September 7, 2018
https://builttosell.com/radio/episode-150/

David Hauser, Founder, Grasshopper
Show date: August 17, 2018
https://builttosell.com/radio/episode-149/

Eric Enge, Founder, Stone Temple Consulting
Show date: August 10, 2018
https://builttosell.com/radio/episode-148/

Sophie Howard, Founder, Aspiring Entrepreneurs
Show date: August 3, 2018
https://builttosell.com/radio/episode-147/

Stephen Heese, Owner, Chris-Craft Corporation
Show date: July 27, 2018
https://builttosell.com/radio/episode-146/

Nathaniel Broughton, Founder, Spread Effect
Show date: July 20, 2018
https://builttosell.com/radio/episode-145/

Ross Hoek, Founder, Impres Enterprises
Show date: July 13, 2018
https://builttosell.com/radio/episode-144/

Gabriel Galvez, Founder, Merger Labs
Show date: July 6, 2018
https://builttosell.com/radio/episode-143/

Julie Nirvelli, Founder, Winking Girl! Foods
Show date: June 29, 2018
https://builttosell.com/radio/episode-142/

Acknowledgments

James Murphy, Founder, Viviscal
Show date: June 15, 2018
https://builttosell.com/radio/episode-141/

Kamal Yadav, Founder, Chemco Industries
Show date: May 25, 2018
https://builttosell.com/radio/episode-140/

Stephanie Leshney, Owner, Ross Organic
Show date: May 18, 2018
https://builttosell.com/radio/episode-139/

Tom Hannon, Owner, FPD
Show date: May 11, 2018
https://builttosell.com/radio/episode-138/

Pete Borum, Owner, Reelio
Show date: May 4, 2018
https://builttosell.com/radio/episode-137/

Steven Harmer, Owner, Blast Radius
Show date: April 27, 2018
https://builttosell.com/radio/episode-136/

Tomas Gorny, Owner, IPOWER 2001
Show date: April 20, 2018
https://builttosell.com/radio/episode-135/

Damien James, Founder, Dimple
Show date: April 6, 2018
https://builttosell.com/radio/episode-134/

Jeffrey Feldberg, Founder, Embanet
Show date: April 4, 2018
https://builttosell.com/radio/episode-133/

Stephen Wells, Founder, Embanet
Show date: April 4, 2018
https://builttosell.com/radio/episode-133/

Tevya Finger, Founder, Luxury Brand Partners
Show date: March 23, 2018
https://builttosell.com/radio/episode-131/

Chris Rezendes, Owner, Impact LABS
Show date: March 21, 2018
https://builttosell.com/radio/episode-130/

Moritz Plassnig, Owner, Cloudship
Show date: March 9, 2018
https://builttosell.com/radio/episode-129/

Harpaul Sambhi, Owner, Careerify
Show date: March 2, 2018
https://builttosell.com/radio/episode-128/

Michael Pedone, Owner, eTrafficJams
Show date: February 23, 2018
https://builttosell.com/radio/episode-127/

Scott Miller, Founder, Miller Restoration
Show date: February 16, 2018
https://builttosell.com/radio/episode-126/

Andy Nulman, Owner, Airborne Mobile
Show date: February 9, 2018
https://builttosell.com/radio/episode-125/

Rich Manders, Owner, iAutomation
Show date: February 2, 2018
https://builttosell.com/radio/episode-124/

Jon Read, Owner, Keet Health
Show date: January 26, 2018
https://builttosell.com/radio/episode-123/

Claude Théoret, Owner, Nexalogy
Show date: January 12, 2018
https://builttosell.com/radio/episode-122/

Courtney Reum, Owner, Veev Vodka
Show date: January 5, 2018
https://builttosell.com/radio/episode-121/

Charles Jolley, Owner, Ozlo
Show date: December 29, 2017
https://builttosell.com/radio/episode-120/

David Fairley, Owner, Hammocks.com
Show date: December 22, 2017
https://builttosell.com/radio/episode-119/

Drew Goodmanson, Owner, Monk Development
Show date: December 4, 2017
https://builttosell.com/radio/episode-118/

Cindy Whitehead, Owner, Sprout Pharmaceuticals
Show date: November 22, 2017
https://builttosell.com/radio/episode-117/

Anthony Lacavera, Owner, Wind Mobile
Show date: November 15, 2017
https://builttosell.com/radio/episode-116/

Dave Ripley, Founder, Glidera
Show date: November 9, 2017
https://builttosell.com/radio/episode-115/

Chris Muench, Founder, C-Labs
Show date: November 2, 2017
https://builttosell.com/radio/episode-114/

Jim McManaman, Founder, Solution One
Show date: October 18, 2017
https://builttosell.com/radio/episode-113/

Etienne Borgeat, Founder, PCO Innovation
Show date: October 11, 2017
https://builttosell.com/radio/episode-112/

Tom Franceski, Co-Owner, DocStar
Show date: October 4, 2017
https://builttosell.com/radio/episode-111/

Hank Goddard, Owner, Mainspring Healthcare Solutions
Show date: September 20, 2017
https://builttosell.com/radio/episode-110/

Sohail Khan, Founder, JV Global Consulting
Show date: September 13, 2017
https://builttosell.com/radio/episode-109/

Jay Steinfeld, Founder, Blinds.com
Show date: September 6, 2017
https://builttosell.com/radio/episode-108/

Dan Martell, Founder, Spheric Technologies
Show date: August 30, 2017
https://builttosell.com/radio/episode-107/

Susan Hrib, Founder, Signum
Show date: August 27, 2017
https://builttosell.com/radio/episode-106/

Terry Lammers, Owner, Tri-County Petroleum
Show date: August 23, 2017
https://builttosell.com/radio/episode-105/

Brian Ferrilla, Founder, Resort Advantage
Show date: August 16, 2017
https://builttosell.com/radio/episode-104/

Randy Ambrosie, President & CEO, 3Macs
Show date: August 9, 2017
https://builttosell.com/radio/episode-103/

Jason Bolt, Founder, Society43
Show date: August 2, 2017
https://builttosell.com/radio/episode-102/

Josh Holtzman, Founder & CEO, American Data Company
Show date: July 19, 2017
https://builttosell.com/radio/episode-101/

Jonathan Jay, CEO, The Dealmakers Academy
Show date: July 12, 2017
https://builttosell.com/radio/episode-100/

Shaun Oshman, Founder, iSupportU
Show date: July 5, 2017
https://builttosell.com/radio/episode-99/

Jill Nelson, Founder, Ruby Receptionists
Show date: June 28, 2017
https://builttosell.com/radio/episode-98/

Joey Redner, Founder, Cigar City Brewing
Show date: June 21, 2017
https://builttosell.com/radio/episode-97/

Ari Ackerman, Founder, Bunk1
Show date: June 14, 2017
https://builttosell.com/radio/episode-96/

Dan Faggella, Founder, Science of Skill
Show date: June 7, 2017
https://builttosell.com/radio/episode-95/

Shelley Rogers, Founder, Admincomm Warehousing
Show date: May 31, 2017
https://builttosell.com/radio/episode-94/

Michele Romanow, Founder, Buytopia
Show date: May 24, 2017
https://builttosell.com/radio/episode-93/

Carl Gould, Founder, Outdoor Imaging
Show date: May 17, 2017
https://builttosell.com/radio/episode-92/

Adam Glickman, Founder, Jumbo Brand Condoms
Show date: May 10, 2017
https://builttosell.com/radio/episode-91/

David Trewern, Founder, DT
Show date: May 3, 2017
https://builttosell.com/radio/episode-90/

Lois Melbourne, Co-Founder, Aquire Solutions
Show date: April 26, 2017
https://builttosell.com/radio/episode-89/

Rocky Romanella, CEO, Unitek
Show date: April 19, 2017
https://builttosell.com/radio/episode-88/

Anthony Amos, Co-Founder, HydroDog
Show date: April 12, 2017
https://builttosell.com/radio/episode-87/

John Arnott, Owner, WaveTwo
Show date: April 5, 2017
https://builttosell.com/radio/episode-86/

Dan Lok, Owner, Table Tennis Master
Show date: March 29, 2017
https://builttosell.com/radio/episode-85/

Dan Green, Founder, The Mortgage Reports
Show date: March 8, 2017
https://builttosell.com/radio/episode-84/

Laura Gisborne, Founder, The Art of Wine
Show date: March 1, 2017
https://builttosell.com/radio/episode-83/

Eric Weiner, Founder, All Occasion Transportation
Show date: February 22, 2017
https://builttosell.com/radio/episode-82/

Nicholas Seet, Founder, Auditude
Show date: February 15, 2017
https://builttosell.com/radio/episode-81/

Ian Ippolito, Founder, Rent a Coder
Show date: February 8, 2017
https://builttosell.com/radio/episode-80/

Peter Shankman, Founder, Help A Reporter Out
Show date: February 1, 2017
https://builttosell.com/radio/episode-79/

Bobby Albert, Owner, The Albert Group of Companies
Show date: January 25, 2017
https://builttosell.com/radio/episode-78/

Julie Pickens, Co-Founder, Boogie Wipes
Show date: January 11, 2017
https://builttosell.com/radio/episode-77/

Bert Martinez, Founder, Accelerator
Show date: January 4, 2017
https://builttosell.com/radio/episode-76/

Rajiv Kumar, Founder, ShapeUp
Show date: December 28, 2016
https://builttosell.com/radio/episode-75/

Stephanie Breedlove, Founder, Breedlove & Associates
Show date: December 21, 2016
https://builttosell.com/radio/episode-74/

Eric Sit, Founder, Detection Technologies
Show date: December 14, 2016
https://builttosell.com/radio/episode-73/

Barry Hinckley, Co-Founder, Bullhorn
Show date: December 7, 2016
https://builttosell.com/radio/episode-72/

Michael Gerber, Founder, E-Myth
Show date: November 30, 2016
https://builttosell.com/radio/episode-71/

Frank Cottle, Investor, Hi-Mark Software
Show date: November 23, 2016
https://builttosell.com/radio/episode-70/

Dan Bradbury, Founder, Business Growth Systems
Show date: November 16, 2016
https://builttosell.com/radio/episode-69/

Mark Stephenson, Founder, Media Edge Communications
Show date: November 9, 2016
https://builttosell.com/radio/episode-61/

Steve Huey, Owner, The Learning House
Show date: November 2, 2016
https://builttosell.com/radio/episode-67/

Joe Saul Sehy, Financial Manager, Ameriprise
Show date: October 26, 2016
https://builttosell.com/radio/episode-66/

Doug Chapiewsky, Founder, CenterPoint Solutions
Show date: October 19, 2016
https://builttosell.com/radio/episode-65/

Manny Fernandez, Founder, HomeBuyingCenter.com
Show date: October 12, 2016
https://builttosell.com/radio/episode-64/

Dr. Frank Gibson, Founder, Sixth Millennium
Show date: October 5, 2016
https://builttosell.com/radio/episode-63/

James Garvey, Founder, Objective Loyalty
Show date: September 28, 2016
https://builttosell.com/radio/episode-62/

Acknowledgments

Mac Lackey, Founder, Kick
Show date: September 21, 2016
https://builttosell.com/radio/episode-61-2/

Dave Will, Founder, Peach New Media
Show date: September 14, 2016
https://builttosell.com/radio/episode-60/

Jim Beach, Founder, American Computer Experience
Show date: September 7, 2016
https://builttosell.com/radio/episode-59/

Andrew Weinreich, Founder, Six Degrees
Show date: August 24, 2016
https://builttosell.com/radio/episode-58/

Laura Steward, Founder, Guardian Angel Computer Services
Show date: August 17, 2016
https://builttosell.com/radio/episode-57/

Rod Drury, Founder, AfterMail
Show date: August 10, 2016
https://builttosell.com/radio/episode-56/

Lara Morgan, Founder, Pacific Direct
Show date: August 3, 2016
https://builttosell.com/radio/episode-55/

John Bodrozic, Co-Founder, Meridian Systems
Show date: July 27, 2016
https://builttosell.com/radio/episode-54/

Mike Glauser, Founder, Northern Lights
Show date: July 20, 2016
https://builttosell.com/radio/episode-53/

Talia Mashiach, Founder, Eved
Show date: July 13, 2016
https://builttosell.com/radio/episode-52/

Josh Latimer, Owner, Birds Beware
Show date: July 6, 2016
https://builttosell.com/radio/episode-51/

Barry Wood, Founder, M&I Door Systems
Show date: June 22, 2016
https://builttosell.com/radio/episode-50/

Mike McCarron, Owner, MSM Transportation
Show date: June 15, 2016
https://builttosell.com/radio/episode-49/

Corey Tansom, Founder & CEO, Imaging Path
Show date: June 8, 2016
https://builttosell.com/radio/episode-48/

Mark Carlson, Founder, Minnesota Mailing Solutions
Show date: June 6, 2016
https://builttosell.com/radio/episode-47/

Carl Silbersky, Founder, Polar Rose
Show date: June 1, 2016
https://builttosell.com/radio/episode-46/

Katherine Hague, Co-Founder, ShopLocket
Show date: May 25, 2016
https://builttosell.com/radio/episode-45/

Dennis Hart, Founder, Apex Media
Show date: May 18, 2016
https://builttosell.com/radio/episode-44/

Kris Jones, Founder, Pepperjam
Show date: May 11, 2016
https://builttosell.com/radio/episode-43/

Nathan Latka, Founder, Heyo
Show date: May 4, 2016
https://builttosell.com/radio/episode-42/

John Bowen, CEO, RWB
Show date: April 27, 2016
https://builttosell.com/radio/episode-41/

John Maddox, Co-Founder, Ten Fast Feet
Show date: April 20, 2016
https://builttosell.com/radio/episode-40/

Julie Cole, Founder, Mabel's Labels
Show date: April 13, 2016
https://builttosell.com/radio/episode-39/

Natalie Susi, Founder, Bare Organic Mixers
Show date: April 6, 2016
https://builttosell.com/radio/episode-38/

Aaron Houghton, Founder, iContact
Show date: March 30, 2016
https://builttosell.com/radio/episode-37/

Ryan Born, Founder, Audio Micro
Show date: March 23, 2016
https://builttosell.com/radio/episode-36/

Jeff Hoffman, Founder, Competitive Technologies
Show date: March 16, 2016
https://builttosell.com/radio/episode-35/

Nick Kellet, Founder, Next Action Technologies
Show date: March 9, 2016
https://builttosell.com/radio/episode-34/

Yvonne Tocquigny, Founder, Tocquigny
Show date: March 2, 2016
https://builttosell.com/radio/episode-33/

Trevor McKendrick, Founder, Salem Software
Show date: February 24, 2016
https://builttosell.com/radio/episode-32/

Stephan Spencer, Founder, Net Concepts
Show date: February 17, 2016
https://builttosell.com/radio/episode-31/

Ian Schoen, Founder, Two Tree International
Show date: February 10, 2016
https://builttosell.com/radio/episode-30/

Alexis Neely, Founder, New Law Business Model
Show date: February 3, 2016
https://builttosell.com/radio/episode-29/

Kim Ades, Founder, Upward Motion
Show date: January 27, 2016
https://builttosell.com/radio/episode-28/

Hampus Jakobsson, Founder, The Astonishing Tribe
Show date: January 20, 2016
https://builttosell.com/radio/episode-27/

Jack Groot, Founder, JP's Coffee Shop
Show date: January 13, 2016
https://builttosell.com/radio/episode-26/

Trent Dyrsmid, Founder, Dyrand Systems
Show date: January 6, 2016
https://builttosell.com/radio/episode-25/

Kevin Kruse, President & Founder, Axiom
Show date: December 16, 2015
https://builttosell.com/radio/episode-24/

Phillip Carson, Founder, Priority Care Health Corporation
Show date: December 9, 2015
https://builttosell.com/radio/episode-23/

Beate Chelette, President & CEO, Beate Works
Show date: December 2, 2015
https://builttosell.com/radio/episode-22/

Cody McLain, Founder, Pacific Host
Show date: November 24, 2015
https://builttosell.com/radio/episode-21/

Mark Selcow, Founder, BabyCenter.com
Show date: November 18, 2015
https://builttosell.com/radio/episode-20/

Erik Huberman, Founder, Swag of the Month
Show date: November 11, 2015
https://builttosell.com/radio/episode-19/

Rick Day, Founder, Daycom Systems
Show date: November 4, 2015
https://builttosell.com/radio/episode-18/

Mark Patey, Founder, Prodigy Engineering
Show date: October 28, 2015
https://builttosell.com/radio/episode-17/

Andrew Yang, Founder, Manhattan GMAT
Show date: October 21, 2015
https://builttosell.com/radio/episode-16/

Derek Sivers, Founder, CD Baby
Show date: October 14, 2015
https://builttosell.com/radio/episode-15/

Walter Bergeron, Founder, Power Control Services
Show date: October 7, 2015
https://builttosell.com/radio/episode-14/

David Phelps, Founder, Gentle Dental
Show date: September 30, 2015
https://builttosell.com/radio/episode-13/

Bobby Martin, Co-Founder, First Research
Show date: September 23, 2015
https://builttosell.com/radio/episode-12/

John Ratliff, Founder, Appletree Answers
Show date: September 16, 2015
https://builttosell.com/radio/episode-11/

Mike Campion, Owner, Killer Shade
Show date: September 9, 2015
https://builttosell.com/radio/episode-10/

Rick Martinez, Founder, MedTrust
Show date: September 2, 2015
https://builttosell.com/radio/episode-9/

Kevin Sullivan, Owner, CCS Digital
Show date: August 26, 2015
https://builttosell.com/radio/episode-8/

Heather Osgood, Co-Founder, Inspired Expos
Show date: August 19, 2015
https://builttosell.com/radio/episode-7/

Jason Swenk, Founder, Solar Velocity
Show date: August 12, 2015
https://builttosell.com/radio/episode-6/

Aaron Walker, Founder, Aaron's Jewelry & Loan
Show date: August 5, 2015
https://builttosell.com/radio/episode-5/

Jeff Davis, Founder, Legal Artworks
Show date: July 29, 2015
https://builttosell.com/radio/episode-4/

Bo Burlingham, Author, *Small Giants: Companies That Choose to Be Great Instead of Big*
Show date: July 22, 2015
https://builttosell.com/radio/episode-3/

Stuart Crane, Founder, DHS Software
Show date: July 15, 2015
https://builttosell.com/radio/episode-2/

Laura Coe, Founder, Litholink
Show date: July 15, 2015
https://builttosell.com/radio/episode-1/

Thank you to the M&A professionals and deal experts who also provided input, including Chris Barnard, Certified Value Builder™ and founder of Marigold Resources; Marla DiCarlo, Certified Value Builder and CEO at Raincatcher; Dr. L. Nolan Duck, M&A advisor and Certified Value Builder at DBG Advisors; George W. Giles III, Certified Value Builder at Intemedior; Geoff Green, Certified Value Builder and the author of *The Smart Business Exit*; Todd McGreevy, Certified Value Builder and co-founder of Marigold Resources; Ed Mysogland, Certified Value Builder and managing partner at Indiana Business Advisors; John J. Roppo, Certified Value Builder; Scott Swim, Certified Value Builder and senior broker at Legacy Mergers & Acquisitions; and Zane Tarence, managing director and partner, Founders Advisors. I'd also like to thank friends and family who suffered through early drafts, including Suzanne Dyment; Sean Hunt; Steve Losty; Ted Matthews; and Emma, Jim, and Wendy Warrillow.

APPENDIX A:
ADDITIONAL RESOURCES

SIGN UP AT BUILTTOSELL.COM

Many of the stories in this book were made possible by the generous owners who shared their stories with me for my podcast called *Built to Sell Radio*. Each week I interview a different business owner and ask them about their exit, probing for what triggered their decision to sell, how their negotiations unfolded, and what they would do differently if they had their business to sell over again. Visit BuiltToSell.com, where you can listen to hundreds of past episodes. Sign up (it's free) and get a new episode every week, a chapter of *Built to Sell*, an e-book called *Famous or Rich: 9 Ways Value Creators Prioritize Wealth Over Recognition*, and all sorts of other goodies.

GET YOUR VALUE BUILDER SCORE AT VALUEBUILDER.COM

Take 10 minutes and complete the Value Builder questionnaire, which will provide an assessment of how your business is performing on the eight factors acquirers look for in a business. Your Value Builder Report will identify parts of your business that will be most attractive to a strategic acquirer and will point out some of the hidden value killers that could be quietly driving down the value of your business.

GET YOUR PRESCORE™ AT PRESCORE.COM

PREScore (or **P**ersonal **R**eadiness to **E**xit Score) is an eight-minute online questionnaire that evaluates your psychological readiness to exit your company. Using an exclusive algorithm developed by analyzing more than 40,000 business owners and conducting more than 200 in-depth interviews with owners who have recently sold, PREScore calculates your exit readiness by identifying your status on each of the four drivers of a satisfying exit. The 12 questions that make up PREScore are often overlooked by business owners, thus leaving them unprepared and in a state of crisis after they make the decision to exit. PREScore helps you identify the at-risk areas and provides personalized recommendations to maximize your odds of a happy and lucrative exit.

READ *BUILT TO SELL*

Built to Sell is a book about how to transform your business into a sellable company. It provides a systematic way to reduce your company's dependence on you, thereby giving you the ultimate poker hand: the choice to make money while you sleep, bring on a partner to run it day-to-day, or sell to the highest bidder.

READ *THE AUTOMATIC CUSTOMER*

As you learned in the pages of this book, acquirers love recurring revenue. It's arguably the most important attribute savvy buyers seek, yet many founders aren't sure how to create an annuity stream of revenue. If you're in an industry where recurring billing is not the norm, *The Automatic Customer* will give you nine subscription models to choose from—meaning that just about any business can create some recurring revenue.

APPENDIX B:
M&A LINGO DECODER

There is a lot of jargon in the world of M&A. Here are a few of the more common terms you may run into.

Accretive acquisition: A deal where the acquisition adds more to the value of the acquiring company than the acquisition cost the acquirer. Imagine a publicly traded company that trades for 12 times EBITDA and that acquires a company for five times EBITDA. Provided the acquiring company's stock does not trade down on the news of the acquisition, the purchase would be deemed as accretive because the profits of the acquired company would be folded into the buyer's business. The earnings the acquirer bought for five times would be worth 12 times in the hands of the acquirer.

Adjusted EBITDA: Earnings before interest, taxes, depreciation, and amortization, adjusted to reflect the profitability of your business in a buyer's hands. Typical adjustments that may drive up reported EBITDA would be things like executive compensation (assuming you're paying yourself more than it would cost to replace you with a general manager), personal travel, automobile expenses, one-time extraordinary expenses (such as a lawsuit), etc.

Basket: Often used in an acquisition agreement, a "basket" provides for a threshold amount of losses/damages incurred because you did not disclose something important prior to closing, after which the acquirer is entitled to compensation.

There are two types of baskets used in M&A transactions. One is a "true deductible," which works like an insurance policy. In other words, there's an amount of money the acquirer needs to lose before they are entitled to compensation. The other type is called a "tipping basket," whereby if a loss exceeds the basket amount, then the acquirer is entitled to compensation for the entire loss—not just the portion that exceeds the deductible.

Let's imagine a scenario where you sell the shares of your company, and at the time of the acquisition you have a $200,000 receivable that you told the acquirer is collectible. If there were a $150,000 true deductible basket in place, and the acquirer was unable to collect the $200,000, they would be entitled to $50,000 of compensation ($200,000 minus $150,000). However, if the agreement stipulated a $150,000 tipping basket, the acquirer would be entitled to the entire amount, because the $200,000 loss exceeds the $150,000 tipping basket.

Confidential information memorandum (CIM): A document prepared by a seller (and their intermediary) that describes the seller's business in enough detail for the acquirer to make an informed decision on pursuing an acquisition. This may also be referred to as a confidential information presentation (CIP).

Consideration: The price an acquirer pays for a business. The most common forms of consideration are cash and stock.

Covenant: A promise to do (or not do) something. Typical covenants you may need to sign are a covenant not to compete directly with your acquirer and/or not hire your current staff in another capacity for a period of time.

Definitive purchase agreement: Unlike a letter of intent, which is usually nonbinding, the definitive purchase agreement is the final agreement signed by both buyer and seller.

Downstroke: The minimum amount of money you stand to make from an acquisition. Let's say you agree to sell your business for $5 million up front and the possibility of another $2 million tied to an earnout. Your downstroke in this example would be $5 million.

Earnout: A scenario where you stand to gain additional consideration (i.e., money) for selling your business if you agree to stay on after selling it. Earnout payments are usually contingent on you hitting specific goals post-sale.

Escrow: An amount of money that is held by a lawyer for a period of time after an M&A transaction. An escrow is set up to deal with any disputes that may arise after the transaction closes.

Indemnification: Literally means "compensation for loss or harm." In an M&A transaction, you might provide indemnification for promises ("reps and warranties") you make in a share or an asset purchase agreement.

Investment thesis: The strategic reason(s) a company may choose to invest in or acquire a business.

Prop deal: Short for "proprietary deal," which describes a situation where the seller is negotiating with one buyer.

Quality of earnings (or "Q of E"): When an acquirer has secured an exclusive position to purchase your business via an LOI, and the transaction is over $1 million or $2 million in value, the acquirer will often hire an outside CPA firm that specializes in reviewing financial documentation, to provide an analysis of your historical EBITDA compared with the values provided in your CIM. A Q of E report can often be a milestone, enabling an acquirer to consider a major portion of their due diligence completed.

Representations and warranties (or "reps and warranties"): These are promises you're making about your company. For example, you might be asked to sign a reps and warranties schedule that, among other things, states you're unaware of any pending legal disputes. If the buyer then comes to learn that you're being sued, and they can prove you were aware of the pending action, they likely will make a claim against money held in escrow. But escrow is only an acquirer's first recourse. If the reps and warranties breach is serious enough, the acquirer may end up suing you.

Re-trading: When one party in a negotiation tries to renegotiate a deal term (often the price) after an agreement in principle has been made.

Teaser: A short (one-to-two-page) document prepared by the seller's intermediary to entice potential acquirers into learning more about a business. A teaser typically is anonymous and is designed to provide enough information to entice an acquirer to sign an NDA in return for a CIM that identifies the seller's company.

Turn: M&A professionals use this term to describe an additional multiple of earnings. For example, imagine you're originally offered four times EBITDA for your business, and your M&A professional got the acquirer to raise their offer to five times EBITDA. The M&A professional would refer to their win as getting you an "extra turn."

INDEX

H

I

J

K

L